RANDY TRAVIS

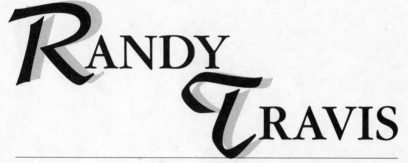

RANDY TRAVIS

King of the New Country
Traditionalists

DON CUSIC

A 2M Communications Production

ST. MARTIN'S PRESS
NEW YORK

DESIGN BY GLEN M. EDELSTEIN

Library of Congress Cataloging-in-Publication Data

Cusic, Don.
    Randy Travis: king of the new country traditionalists / Don Cusic
        p.   cm.
    ISBN 0-312-04412-7
    1. Travis, Randy.   2. Country musicians—Biography.   I. Title.
ML420.T76C9   1990
782.42164'2'092—20
    [B]   89-78017
                                                                   CIP
                                                                   MN

First Edition

10 9 8 7 6 5 4 3 2 1

ACKNOWLEDGMENTS

In gathering information for this book I would like to thank Kate Mangum, Bruce Curlee, Jackie Hill Austin, David Maddox, Evelyn Shriver, Charlie Monk, John Hobbs, John Harper, Kyle Lehning, Martha Sharp, Stan Byrd, Keith Stegall, Jeff Davis, Ann Tant, Stan Byrd, Tommy Goldsmith, Robert Oermann, Nick Hunter, Eddie Reeves, Jerry Bailey, Lonnie Webb, Bill Ivey, Bob Pinson, John Rumble, Hazel Smith, Keith Bilbrey, John Sturdivant, Michael McCall, Patsy Austin Griffin, Junior Godwin, Hilda Ross, Sherry Robin, and Kathy Haight for sharing their time, views, and information with me.

I would also like to thank the Country Music Foundation for their excellent facility and staff, including Jay Orr, Darlene Reger, Becky Bell, and especially Ronnie Pugh; The Nashville Network; the Center for Popular Music at Middle Tennessee State University, especially Ellen Garrison and Sarah Long; the Todd Library at Middle Tennessee State University, especially Betty McFall; the Union County Library in Monroe, North Carolina; the Marshville Public Library; the Charlotte Public Library; the courthouse staffs in Monroe, Wadesboro, and Charlotte, North Carolina, Ashland City and Nashville, Tennessee, and Chesterfield, South Carolina; Warner Brothers Records; and Kelly Gattis and the Country Music Association.

My work and life has been made much easier by Geoff Hull, the Department Chairman of the Recording Industry Management program at MTSU, and I owe him a great deal of gratitude. I also owe a great debt to historian, folklorist, and friend Charles Wolfe for information, advice, and sharing his resources. Jim Neal at MTSU was most valuable in helping with problems with my computer.

I must thank my agent, Madeleine Morel, and the good folks at St. Martin's, particularly editor Jim Fitzgerald and his trusty sidekick, J. P. Olsen.

Finally, I must thank Jackie for keeping the home fires burning and tolerating some long working hours as well as Delaney, Jesse, Eli, and Alex for taking my mind off this book and transferring it to more important matters when I arrived home.

Some men are born great, some achieve greatness, and some have greatness thrust upon them.

Shakespeare, *Twelfth Night*

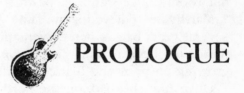 PROLOGUE

U.S. Route 74 runs southeast from Charlotte, North Carolina, through Monroe and on to Marshville. It has three lanes until it reaches the Charlotte city limit, then becomes a two-lane highway. The young bucks drive too fast and reckless, especially on Friday nights, as they race each other, the traffic, or some inner drive. It is the nature of age, I suppose, that when you're young the world can't go fast enough, but as you get older you spend more time trying to tell it to slow down.

It's about thirty miles from Charlotte to Marshville, through gently rolling hills of the Piedmont plateau, and after you pass Monroe, the seat of Union County, there's Wingate, then some farmland with a few stores scattered along the side of the road, and then Marshville.

Driving into Marshville you see a sign, "Marshville, Home of Randy Travis, Country Music's Finest." It is a big sign, easy to read, bordered in blue, and mounted on a brick frame. Appropriately, the radio was playing a Randy Travis song, "Deeper Than the Holler," when I first passed that sign.

At a light, another sign, announcing "Business District," points to the left, and a turn there carries you into downtown Marshville, a small town of around three thousand people, with several streets of stores—a city hall, some restaurants, a women's dress shop, a print and frame shop, a one-room police station, a pawn shop.

Marshville achieved some fame—or perhaps notoriety—several years back when Steven Spielberg brought a cast of thousands here to film *The Color Purple*, a movie about growing up poor and black in the South.

Olive Branch Road, on the north side of town, is a two-lane blacktop that runs north, winding through farmland. Driving along this road another song comes on the radio—"Like Father, Like Son," written by Paul Overstreet and Don Schlitz, who have written a number of Randy's big hits—and I can't help but wonder if there is any significance in hearing this now.

Out several miles past the Marshville Municipal Park, just past a clump of pines bordered by a fence with some horses, is the house where Randy Travis grew up—a neat, white house, one story, with a gravel drive. Here is where Randy's parents, Bobbie Rose and Harold Traywick, live. To the left is another house, where his grandmother lives, and across the street is a barn and some turkey houses.

Bobbie Rose and Randy look a lot alike. She has dark hair, dark eyes, and a square jaw. As I talk with her in the evening twilight, she is quiet and polite; it is obvious where Randy inherited his inner calm and shyness. "No, Harold isn't here right now," she says. "The best time to get with him is early in the morning, before he gets out with the horses." I thank her and head back to town.

The next morning at eight I knock on the front door

again. Harold comes out the side door, and I walk toward him and meet him in the driveway.

Harold Traywick is a tall man—built much like Randy—with thinning hair and a tanned, ruddy complexion. It is obvious he has spent a lot of time outdoors. He moves forcefully, a taut expression on his face, and you can sense an inner tension in him, like he's wound up tight. I introduce myself, and he lashes out.

"Who the hell gave you the right to do a book about my boy?" he asks in a belligerent challenge.

"Well, you do what you do," I say, smiling, "and I write books."

"If anybody's going to write a book about Randy, I'll do it myself." There is no humor in his voice or demeanor. His body seems to tighten under his neat blue shirt.

"Are you planning to do one?" I venture.

"That's none of your damn business," he snaps.

I can see the way this conversation is heading. The terms "laid back" or "easygoing" would not apply to Harold Traywick. He moves closer and points his finger.

"Now you see that damn road?" he says. "Well, you better get on it."

It is obvious that this is not a man to reason with. There is a violence about him you can feel in his presence. I turn, and as I head toward my car, I listen for a click, hoping he has left his gun inside the house.

"I ought to blow your g——m ass away," he barks, his hands in fists as I open the door. I get in my car, start it, and put it in reverse. As I back out of the driveway he takes a step or two toward me, glares, and yells, "Put that in your f——n' book."

CHAPTER 1

*M*arshville is filled with good, upright, law-abiding citizens. They are fine people, hardworking, unpretentious, the kind who are always ready to lend a helping hand to a stranger or a friend. These folks are scared of Harold Traywick. And most are pretty fed up with him, too.

During the past twenty years Harold Traywick has created a reign of terror with his drinking, fighting, shooting, and threatening people in and around the area. One of the results is that people will talk about Harold, but don't want their names used for fear of reprisal.

A man who has known Harold all his life uses him as a lesson: "Harold Traywick is a smart man, a good business man. But he's done himself in with that drinking. At one time, he was building some big-priced houses in Charlotte and other houses all around here. And he had money too. At one time, Harold could walk in any store and buy whatever it was he saw. And he bought those kids just about anything

1

and everything they wanted. But then he lost it all—even lost his house and land. That's what that liquor will do to you."

An old family friend has a look of sadness in her eyes when she says, "Nobody ever has anything good to say about Harold. He just doesn't have a good name. Now that's sad."

But there is one longtime friend who will come to his defense. She says, "Harold Traywick wasn't always like this. He used to be a real sweet man. But that drinking and fighting . . ." She trails off. So what happened? She pauses, then states, "I think Harold's mama spoiled him. He was the youngest and the last one at home, and she just spoiled him rotten. Whatever he said went. He run that family. His daddy, Mr. Bruce, was a real nice man, but I think even he was scared of Harold. His mama still lives right beside him, and she's the sweetest lady you'd ever want to meet. So's Bobbie Rose."

Harold's drinking and fighting have certainly not helped his personal relations with the good folks in Marshville. But that isn't what ruined him financially. It was the turkeys that done that. And just about everybody in Marshville will tell you that story:

"Harold went into business with Armour to raise turkeys, and he built a couple of big turkey barns. The first problem came when a man with Armour in charge of overseeing how farmers were doing discovered Harold was taking some of the turkey feed Armour was supplying and giving it to his hogs. He called Harold on the carpet for that and reported it to Armour. Harold went over to this guy's trailer and shot out all the windows in the man's car. The man, he was in the trailer.

"Then Armour went out of business, and Harold tried to raise those turkeys by himself and couldn't do it. It was just too expensive—it takes a lot of money to raise that many turkeys.

"So he went under, lost everything. And they auctioned off his property. He had guns threatening everybody—the auctioneer, the judges, anybody who came to the auction. There was some people wouldn't come to that auction—scared to come—'cause Harold Traywick was threatening to shoot everybody."

That was the low point for Harold and Bobbie Rose—August 16, 1982, when their home was auctioned off for fifty thousand dollars on the front steps of the Union County Courthouse in Monroe. They moved into a trailer, "and Bobbie Rose just cried over the phone," recalls a friend.

The place was bought by North Carolina Savings and Loan, and a friend of Harold's became trustee. This friend agreed to hold the property until Harold raised the necessary money, then sell it back to him. "That's the only thing that saved Harold from killing somebody," a family friend remembers. "Harold knew he hadn't lost it forever, thought he could get it back."

The Traywicks managed to buy back their property in 1985. Later, when Randy began making money as an entertainer, he sent money home to help with repairs and refurbishing.

"Randy fixed that place up for them—it had gotten pretty run down," says a Marshvillian. "And fixed up some other stuff around there, too—some of the other buildings. Randy's done all right by his parents."

Harold Traywick has a string of arrests going back twenty years, most of them related to alcohol: DWI, public drunkenness, assaulting an officer, discharging a firearm in occupied property, communicating threats, injury to personal property, and simple assault. He is well known to the police in the area, having had regular confrontations with them during the years.

Harold has long been known as someone wild and woolly, rough and rowdy and ready to fight. And he still drinks his Crown Royal and gets carried away sometimes. But lately he seems to have withdrawn some, "probably because he knows everybody's had their fill of him," observes another Marshville resident. "The Traywicks pretty much stay to themselves these days. Harold messes around with those horses out there, but mostly he stays close to the house."

The librarian in Marshville says that Harold rides his horse into town and stops by to see if there are any new articles about Randy. "He wants every article about Randy," she says. "And he brings his grandson in for books sometimes."

Bobbie Rose has purportedly told close friends that her hands are tied, there's nothing she can do. She seems to accept Harold with a quiet resolve, her cool demeanor a marked contrast to Harold's hot blood and feistiness. One of her friends says, "I guess she's a saint. I don't know how she's put up with all that. And this is the twentieth century! I'd of left that man a long time ago. Ain't no reason for a woman to put up with doings like that now. But Bobbie Rose stays."

Another friend quickly counters, "You don't know what's inside other people, what they're thinking. Bobbie Rose couldn't just leave those kids when they were coming along. And she loves that man—loves the ground he walks on." The other women nod in silent agreement.

Meanwhile, Bobbie Rose still works every day at the textile mill in Monroe, where she weighs pot holders and oven mitts and packs them for shipping. "I think she's the only white woman who works there," says a longtime friend.

One recent story that a family friend of the Traywicks tells is particularly revealing. She states, "The TV people from Charlotte came out here and interviewed Bobbie Rose on television, and she said they weren't going to see Randy at the awards show because they couldn't get tickets. Now, I wouldn't have told that on the television. You know Randy could get them tickets if he wanted to. But can you imagine turning Harold Traywick loose at a nationally televised awards show? Lawd, lawd."

There might not be much to see in a small town, but there's a lot to hear. And just about everybody in Marshville has something to say about Harold Traywick. Unfortunately, as one states, "Ain't none of it good." Still, everyone has to reckon with Harold Traywick because he still lives there and because he's the father of Randy Travis, who grew up in Marshville and is now one of the biggest country music stars of all time.

 CHAPTER 2

*A*lexander Pinkney Traywick was born October 9, 1836, in Anson County. His father was Berry Traywick, and his mother the former Martha High. Pinkney married Betsy Little in 1858; Brown Low (or Brownlow) Traywick was born in 1862. In 1883 Brownlow married Jane Bass (born in 1863), and Alexander Bruce Traywick was born September 24, 1899. Bruce Traywick married Maud Etta Davis on November 15, 1921; they had three children: Irene, Ralph, and Harold Bruce Traywick, their youngest, born March 31, 1933.

The Traywicks have lived in the same area for over 150 years. They have lived in either Peachland or Marshville, two small towns only about ten miles apart but, because of the boundary line, in different counties.

The area itself has gone through major changes since it was first inhabited by the Waxhaw indians. Scottish-Irish settlers from Pennsylvania were the first whites to move there, around 1750. Later, around 1775, German settlers came. There were some Revolutionary War skirmishes in the area—Burford's Massacre occurred in South Carolina about six miles south of Union County, and Cornwallis marched up part of the Rocky River Road in Union County.

Cotton began to be a dominate crop around 1800, and plantations soon dominated the economy. Tobacco was introduced by German farmers around 1820. The Civil War ended the dominance of plantations, and the Great Depression ended the dominance of cotton. Tobacco was virtually eliminated by the end of the nineteenth century until the period from 1925 to 1937, when it had a brief revival.

In 1842 Union County was created out of parts of Mecklenburg and Anson counties. The Seaboard Railway was completed in 1874 with stations in Marshville, Wingate, Monroe, and a number of other towns, providing transportation to the outside world. The use of convict labor to grade, straighten, and stabilize roads by "rocking" (covering with rocks) began in 1895; hard surfacing the roads began in 1949.

The area has always been dominated by farms, although a gold rush occurred in the early nineteenth century. At one time there were over forty gold mines, and one mine reportedly produced over $750,000 worth of gold. In the 1850 census, more people were engaged in gold mining than anything else except farming. But by World War II the gold mining had stopped.

During Reconstruction an attempt was made to increase manufacturing in the South. For Union County, this meant a number of textile mills in and around the area.

Though there were no Civil War battles in Marshville or Monroe, the area lost a number of young men in the war—248 of the 1,769 who served for the Confederacy.

The county had some race problems in 1957, when ten blacks were refused admittance into a municipal swimming pool, and a race riot in 1961, when three blacks allegedly kidnapped a white couple. By the early sixties, though, the schools were finally integrated, ending the "separate but equal" school systems.

In the first census in 1850 there were 8,018 whites, 1,982 slaves, and 51 free blacks in Union County; by 1900 the population had reached 27,156. The census for 1960 shows 5,232 persons in Marshville, 315 of them under five years old. Monroe had 18,334 inhabitants, and Union County had 44,670.

There was some hint of prosperity by 1960, when 57 percent of the homes had telephones and farmland was worth an average of $139.14 an acre.

The 1950s were the Eisenhower years and the coming of age for Harold Traywick and Bobbie Rose Tucker, both of whom had been born during the Great Depression and spent their childhood years under the shadow of World War II. Each had had an early marriage that did not last. Both divorces were final by the end of 1956—a time when divorces were not as socially acceptable as they have become since.

Harold and Bobbie Rose were married November 16, 1957, just over the state line in Chesterfield, South Carolina. The ceremony was performed by the probate judge at the courthouse at 7:30 P.M.

In the spring their first child, Ricky Harold, was born, and almost exactly a year after that—on May 4, 1959—Randy Bruce Traywick was born in Memorial Hospital in Monroe at 6:14 A.M., weighing seven pounds, one and a half ounces. He was delivered by Dr. C. A. Bolt. At this time, Harold was twenty-six and Bobbie Rose was twenty-one.

Four other children followed: Rose Mary in 1961, David in 1962, Linda Sue in 1964, and Dennis in 1968.

The family settled into their home on Olive Branch Road, and Harold began building houses after first working in meat packaging. He built a number of houses in the 1960s and 1970s, buying some land, putting up a house, and then selling it. He built houses in Marshville, Peachland, and Charlotte.

On the day Randy Travis was born the music industry held its first Grammy Awards ceremony in Hollywood, California. There was only one award for country music; the Kingston Trio won it for "Tom Dooley."

The number-one country song that week was "White Lightning" by George Jones. Others on the chart included Jim Reeves, George Morgan, Johnny Horton, Skeeter Davis, Johnny Cash, Don Gibson, Kitty Wells, Webb Pierce, Faron Young, Eddy Arnold, Marty Robbins, Porter Wagoner, Ernest Tubb, Bill Anderson, Hank Thompson, and Ray Price.

(Later that year, in November, the second Grammy Awards were televised. The country music award went to Johnny Horton for "The Battle of New Orleans," a major pop success as well. In addition to Horton's classic, the big country song that year was "El Paso" by Marty Robbins.)

The Monroe *Enquirer* of Monday, May 4, 1959, carried the headline "Negro Woman Dies After Being Struck by Auto Near Wingate." Local elections were scheduled the next day for Marshville. A local-boy-made-good, John Tsitouris, was set to pitch for the Kansas City A's against the Boston Red Sox. Numerous sales ads reminded readers that Mother's Day was Sunday, May 10. The paper also carried a notice of the proclamation of National Music Week, May 3–10, "to bring attention to the dynamic influence of music in everyday living."

A movie theater in Monroe ran an advertisement that read, "Every man in Union County wants to see Bardot and every woman should find out why." The movie was *That Naughty Girl* starring Brigitte Bardot. Admission was seventy-five cents for adults, with children free. Another ad showed Marilyn Monroe and her bosom buddies in *Some*

Like It Hot. There was also a notice that Walt Disney's *The Shaggy Dog* would be there soon. (The big movie that year would be *Ben-Hur.*)

There were two television stations in Monroe: WBTV and WSOC. That Monday, "I Love Lucy" was on at 11:00 A.M.; that evening, you could watch "Death Valley Days" at 7:00, "U.S. Marshall" at 7:30, "The Texan" at 8:00, choose between "Father Knows Best" and "Tales of Wells Fargo" at 8:30, and choose between "Danny Thomas" and "Peter Gunn" at 9:00.

Saturday morning television consisted of shows like "The Little Rascals," "The Cisco Kid," "Roy Rogers," "Captain Kangeroo," "Howdy Doody," "Mighty Mouse," "Circus Boy," and "Heckle and Jeckle." On Saturday nights at 7:30 you could watch Dick Clark, at 8:00 Perry Como, at 9:00 Lawrence Welk, at 9:30 "Have Gun Will Travel," and at 10:00 see "Gunsmoke."

In news of the world, 1959 is the year Alaska and Hawaii became states, the Saint Lawrence Seaway in Canada was opened, Charles de Gaulle was proclaimed president of France, Fidel Castro led a revolution and took over leadership in Cuba, and the Russian spaceships Lunik II and III photographed the "back" side of the moon.

In the music industry, it was three months after the plane crash that killed Buddy Holly, Richie Valens, and the Big Bopper. A major investigation about payola would eventually shake up the music industry. Elvis was serving in the Army in Germany, although his song "Are You Lonesome Tonight" was on the charts.

It was a time when the rock and roll revolution was turning into the trend of record labels signing pretty young men to sing for teenagers, while the press and some leaders proclaimed that rock and roll wouldn't last.

CHAPTER 3

*H*arold Traywick always had an intense love for country music. He played the guitar, sang, and wrote songs. "I remember Harold Traywick having tons of songs," one friend states. "He would say that he'd sent some to Ernest Tubb or Patsy Cline or somebody like that. That's when they were big stars."

Harold even made a record of two of his songs, "A Lonely Shadow" backed with "The Reason I Came," that received some airplay in Monroe. Occasionally he would get up on a stage in a club and sing.

During the early 1960s, when Harold was doing well financially, building houses, he did not hesitate to shower material gifts on his children. In fact, he admits that "from the time they were four years old they all had horses—all six of them. They all had Honda motorcycles and go-carts, and then I got them guitars and music lessons."

He sent them all over to Kate Mangum to learn how play.

Mrs. Mangum lives about five miles from the Traywicks in New Salem. Her small home, situated beside a dusty road, was the site of music lessons for about sixty students back then.

Kate was well known in the area for her guitar playing. Her uncle, Homer Dye (he later changed his name to Homer Briarhopper), was one of the Briarhoppers, the renowned North Carolina group. Her son, Jimmy Mangum, is now a musician and studio owner living in Jacksonville, Florida.

Kate loved country music and knew how to play rhythm guitar. She taught the Traywick boys—first Ricky and Randy, then David. Her lessons began with her teaching the chords for the key of G: G, C, and D. The Traywick boys would usually come over on Wednesdays, although sometimes they had to change because their mother had to work late. The one-hour lesson would consist of learning chords and then playing along while Mrs. Mangum led a country song. These lessons began in 1967, when Randy was eight, and lasted for three years.

"There was no reason for the lessons to last that long," she says. "They caught on so quick. But their momma and daddy wanted to make sure they'd stay with it, so they kept coming over."

Mrs. Mangum remembers Ricky being a better guitar player than Randy, but Ricky wanted to play rock and roll. Randy was more easygoing, she states. "Ricky would say 'I don't like that song. I don't want to play it.' But Randy would always say, 'She's our teacher and we need to learn what she's showing us.'"

She also remembers something else about Randy. "Soon after we started lessons, he wanted me to show him how to play 'I Saw the Light,'" she says. "So I showed him and he sang it, and I said 'You sing that as good as Hank Williams.' 'You really think so?' he asked. And I said 'If you work hard you could be like that, too.'" Randy was impressed and a little awed. He learned the song in G because "that was a good key for his voice."

She recalls that story as she tells about going to see Randy in his first big concert at the Charlotte Coliseum, opening for George Jones, when the band used "I Saw the Light" as a theme song.

Harold raised his boys on country music and built a twenty-by-forty-foot music room in the back of his house, complete with a stage at one end. On weekends he would invite friends over. A longtime friend remembers that "Bobbie Rose would fix a catfish stew or something, and he would play and sing and he would get those boys up to play and sing. They were just as cute as could be."

In 1968, when Randy was nine, he and Ricky played their first public gig—a fiddler's convention at the Marshville Elementary School. In the following years the two boys, joined later by brother David on bass, played a number of other fiddler's conventions, where they usually entered the "sixteen and under" talent contests. Harold booked them into other appearances as well: a benefit for the Burnsville Fire and Rescue Squad; the Indian Trail Jaycee's Battle of the Bands at Sun Valley High School; an appearance on the Sandhill Opry in Pageland, South Carolina; another at the VFW; and a country and western show sponsored by the Peachland Women's Club.

In the late 1960s and early 1970s Harold spent a lot of money on those boys, buying them guitars and cowboy outfits from Lebo's in Charlotte. Randy still has the Gibson with a white dove on the pick guard that Harold bought him to learn on.

Though the boys did not win that first fiddler's contest they entered, by the time Randy was eleven he and Ricky were routinely winning first prize in the talent contests. Harold compiled scrapbooks from stories in local papers about the boys. He still has them and updates them with new articles about Randy. He has said about those early contests, "They were serious. They went to win. I was too. In fact, I would pick out the songs and tell them what to sing, and they would do it."

Harold, who is quick to take credit for Randy's success, states, "I know Randy ain't forgot it, but I've stopped him lots of times in practice when he'd do a song wrong and make him start over—right in the middle or wherever he was at. If he hit a note wrong or done it wrong I'd stop him, because I think I knew as much about country music then as anybody did." He adds, "If he hadn't started when he did and I hadn't kept him at it like I did, he wouldn't be singing today."

During this time, Ricky and Randy had their first recording sesson, financed by their father. At Arthur Smith's studio in Charlotte they cut a demo of George Jones's tune "Grand Tour."

When Randy was nine Harold built the big room on the back of his home that served as a private lounge as well as a music room. Some of the trophies and ribbons the boys won still fill a shelf there. Harold states, "At that time, I thought they could be like the Everly Brothers. I had a jukebox in the right-hand corner and one as you came in the door on the left-hand side. And there's the dance floor, kitchen, and bathroom."

But people around Marshville tell another side of the story, too. One friend states, "Randy was always scared of his daddy. All those kids were. Terrified is a better word. Absolutely terrified!"

And someone else recalls, "Those boys didn't always want to play. But that was always Harold's thing—making people do stuff that he wanted them too. 'Course, now that Randy's a big star, it looks like it turned out all right."

A family friend who watched the boys play during that

time remembers that "those boys went to fiddler's conventions, and they'd usually win the talent contests. But if they didn't, their daddy would be right up in the judge's faces, at their necks, just giving them a going over. I'd try to tell him, 'You can't win everything.' But Harold's just a big bully. That's what he is."

CHAPTER 4

When you ask about the Traywick kids in Marshville, most people will slowly shake their head and say, "Those kids had a hard life." That phrase and that reaction come up over and over again. The problem again is Harold's drinking. Sometimes he'd get a little too full of fight, and maybe he'd take it out on those closest to him.

"All his kids are terrified of him. Still are," says one Marshvillian who knows the family. "I remember one night Randy hiding in a neighbor's closet while his daddy kept calling, looking for him. Ricky ran away once, and when he came back, he didn't come to Harold's house. He went to a friend's house and wanted to stay there. She made him call his momma, 'cause his momma hadn't seen him, before she'd feed him. So he did, and later Harold and Bobbie Rose came over and got him."

It's hard not to run into someone in Marshville who went to school with Randy or one of his brothers or sisters. And most, though proud of that fact, will admit when pressed, "It's hard to believe he's such a big star. I mean, we know the truth."

The "truth" is that Randy was a less-than-average student and nobody expected too much out of him. Then, the older he got the wilder he got, and nobody likes to have trouble-makers like that around. A young man with a lot of fire in him can burn up a small town in a hurry, and the Traywick boys wore out Marshville pretty bad.

Indeed, a lot of people saw those boys back then and wished somehow they'd just leave town. And in a strange way, that's what happened to one of those high-spirited, hell-raising young troublemakers—but he turned out to be a country music star, a winner of major awards, and the pride and joy of Marshville.

People there have mixed feelings about Randy and his brothers.

Why were the Traywick boys so wild? Well, most folks in Marshville begin by saying that's just the way some young men are. They have to get it out of their systems. Bobbie Rose, trying to explain it, has said they "just had to sow their wild oats." But after that initial explanation, most admit that the boys were following in their daddy's footsteps. They raised hell because Harold Traywick raised hell; it was a way of life for them, a way they learned firsthand.

Of course, life wasn't composed entirely of shenanigans. Randy would spend long hours riding his horse, Buckshot. Sometimes the whole family would saddle up and ride to-gether, covering twenty miles through the woods and fields around their home. There was a peacefulness about horse-back riding that brought a closeness to the family. Randy would also spend hours with his best friend, Tim Griffin, who lived a few miles up the road from him. The two would talk, ride horses, and, later, cruise around together.

*　　*　　*

Randy started getting hauled into court when he was a juvenile, and by the time he turned sixteen he was ready to start filling up files in the criminal clerk's office. Quitting school in the ninth grade, when he was fifteen, just seemed to give him more time to get into trouble.

Around that time Randy stole his brother Ricky's car from the parking lot at Forest Hills High School and headed to Pageland—about fifteen miles south of Marshville in South Carolina—with a buddy. They were flagged down by a policeman, and Randy pulled off onto a side road. The policeman asked what was wrong. Randy replied that the car was hung up in gear, then took off for about another fifteen miles. He lost control of the car after being clocked at 135 miles an hour, spun around, and went five hundred feet backward through a corn field before stopping.

Harold had bought this car, a 1968 396 Chevelle, for Ricky. After the wreck he sold it and bought Ricky a 1974 Cutlass.

The year 1976 saw Randy and his buddies get into a whole pack of trouble. In January they broke into the Nicey Grove Church in Wingate, where they held a beer-drinking party. In February he was arrested for DWI and trying to elude a police officer. In April he was arrested for public drunkenness. In July he threw a brick through the window of Pruitt Phifer's store in Marshville, then he and Ricky stole some pocketknives and Timex watches. In November Randy was arrested for violating his probation; in December for DWI, disorderly conduct, and driving on a revoked license; and in January 1977 for attempted larceny.

The Traywick boys were well known to the local police. It wasn't unusual to see them—especially on a weekend—at two or three in the morning, hanging out or cruising around. And then there were the inevitable trips to jail in the middle of the night to bail them out. Harold says that

Randy and Ricky "got locked up so much they'd take turns calling home for me to come get them out. I must have bailed them out fifty times at two in the morning."

Though Harold usually bailed them out, it was their mother who accompanied them to the courtroom. She was always the one to supply the tender loving care, to be there trying to soothe things over. She confessed to friends that she was worried about her boys; Randy, Ricky, and David were all developing long criminal records. She told one friend, "I hope one of them turns out all right." And she also told this friend, "If one does turn out good, I think it'll be Randy."

On Randy's seventeenth birthday—May 4, 1976—he was sitting in the Union County courtroom facing charges of public drunkenness. Like his daddy, Randy was inclined to get into trouble when he got tanked up.

The simple fact was that putting liquor into a Traywick is like pouring gasoline on a fire. He was in trouble and getting deeper. By the time he was arrested in January 1977 it was already getting too late. His lawyer had told him there was little hope of avoiding prison; he could expect to get five years. It didn't seem like a good way to spend 1,826 days.

There weren't many options left. Most of his friends and running buddies were heading in the same direction, and staying in Marshville meant more of the same. He was armed for life with an eighth-grade education—just like his daddy.

Only one thing might change all this and turn his life around—country music. There were no alternatives; at this point it was either singing in bars or sitting behind them. Only Randy didn't realize this quite yet.

CHAPTER 5

*I*t is easy to say that Randy would be singing country music no matter what, even if he had never left Marshville when he did. And no doubt that's true—but he would probably be singing in a prison band.

The Traywick boys had continued playing country music through their teenage years. Randy remembers playing honky-tonks at fourteen: "I was playing in them before I was old enough to go in them."

He also remembers that "the worst place we played was probably Peyton Place. There was a lady one time who fought like any man you'd ever seen. It took three policemen to get her out of there. She was rough. I was only, like, fourteen, and I said, 'I can't believe this.' She was having too much fun, I guess. They finally just threw her down on the pool table, handcuffed her behind her back, and more or less carried her out. She was something."

During the coldest winter in years—the early months of

1977—the Traywicks heard about a talent contest at Country City USA, a nightclub in Charlotte, while listening to John Harper's morning show on WSOC. Harold got Randy and Ricky in the car and drove them to Charlotte, where they climbed up on stage like so many other hopefuls and sang. By the time the contest ended, there would be 119 other contestants competing for a first prize of one hundred dollars in cash and some time in Dimension Recording Studio.

The contest consisted of an eight-week series of semifinal rounds where the less talented were weeded out, culminating in a final round where one winner was picked. The rounds took place on Tuesday nights—an off night for the club—in order to drum up business. The contest was the brainchild of the manager and part owner of the club, a lady by the name of Lib Hatcher.

That first night, Ricky played lead guitar while Randy played rhythm and sang. Lib remembers it well. "I'll never forget it," she says. "There was a little table near the stage where I'd sit a lot and work on some papers. When I heard Randy, I just sort of dropped the papers and thought, 'This is something special.'"

Lib also remembers the impression he made then. "He was so shy that he wouldn't talk to anybody. He'd sing his song, then hang his head and sort of get down from the stage. He wouldn't even say thank you. But he would talk to me, and after we closed at night he'd get the guitar and he'd sing while we were waiting for the girls to clean up the place."

When the night of the finals rolled around, at the end of April, Randy stood on the stage alone—Ricky was doing time at a juvenile detention center, where he would spend a year. Meanwhile, not only did Randy win the contest that night, he also won a patron and future manager as well.

Afterward, Randy was at the club one night when he confessed to Lib that he was facing a jail term. The court date was set for June. According to Randy's story, he was out with some buddies roaring and swarming the area. It was January and freezing, and Randy found himself left out in the cold and walking back toward home. He spotted a pickup truck in a driveway, hot-wired it, and drove home, intending to take the truck back later after he had woken up and thawed out. But the truck's owner reported it missing and Randy was arrested.

Lib Hatcher is, if anything, a woman of action. She lost no time in going into action on Randy's behalf, and showed Randy she cared about him as a person as well as a performer. She told him she believed in him, and he responded by listening to and following her advice—something he had not done for anyone else. The result was the ending of Randy Traywick of Marshville and the beginning of Randy Travis, country music star.

Randy did not plan on moving in with the Hatchers—and Lib did not plan on it either—but he ended up there one night after being left stranded at the club with no ride home at closing time. Since he had nowhere else to go, Lib invited him to the Hatcher's mobile home in Huntland, just outside the city limits west of Charlotte. He never went back to Marshville to live again.

Lib gave him a regular job singing at her club—a job that also entailed helping out in general. She and John Harper, the popular disc jockey for WSOC in Charlotte who worked at Country City USA as an announcer three nights a week, went down to the Monroe Courthouse and convinced the judge that Randy Traywick should not go to jail. The reason: Randy now had a new job and a new lease on life.

This meant altering the terms of Randy's probation to allow him to live and work in Charlotte instead of staying within the confines of Union County. It also meant that Lib would have custody of the teenager, taking him out of Harold Traywick's home and domain.

The judge was convinced but a little skeptical. He told Randy at the hearing that he would allow the custody, the move, and the change in his probation. But if things continued to go wrong, the next time Randy appeared in that courtroom he should bring his toothbrush, because he would be getting no more second chances—he would be headed for prison if this didn't work.

The probation officer eyed him and said she would be watching closely—just waiting for the inevitable slipup. Bad blood never changes.

It was a sobering thought to seventeen-year-old Randy Traywick. And it marked a turning point in his life. By June 1977 all the details had been wrapped up and Randy was living and working in Charlotte, staying with the Hatchers and out of trouble.

CHAPTER 6

*M*ary Elizabeth Robertson was born in Kernersville, North Carolina, to Hill and Mary Robertson on April 15, 1941. After graduating from high school in 1959—the same year Randy was born—she took an office job with the Youngblood Trucking Company in nearby Winston-Salem. She soon left and began working as a waitress for Lawrence Staley. After working at Staley's restaurant in Winston-Salem she moved to Charlotte to work in another of his restaurants.

Lib has always been energetic, a hard worker. She began waiting tables at the Pony Restaurant in Kernersville, which her parents leased and where her mother was the manager. Here she would work each morning from 6:00 to 8:30, then go to school until lunch, when she came back and worked as cashier. After school, she would be working again until closing time. She was a compulsive worker, always doing something, more driven to working than studying.

In order to buy her first car when she was sixteen she took in ironing—against her father's wishes—to earn the money. Within a year she was able to purchase a used Mercury.

Hill Robertson states, "I can tell you the first dollar she got and how she got it. One day I was going down to my mother's house down a dirt road—there wasn't much blacktop then. She was probably two years old. I was holding her hand, and she said, 'Wait a minute, Daddy.' She saw a corner of that dollar bill sticking up on the side of the road. She saw the number 'one' and the green. I think that's what got her started."

Lib also grew up loving country music. Her first trip to the Grand Ole Opry occurred when she "was probably five years old," she says. Later, she visited the Opry several times while spending the summer with friends near Nashville.

After Lawrence Staley died, Lib went to work for Angelo Pappas at the Driftwood restaurant. She met Frank Lafon Hatcher, who worked for a pipeline contractor, and they moved in together. They were married October 21, 1967, in Charlotte by a justice of the peace. It was his second marriage, her first.

Never one to do anything halfway, Lib got into gardening because she needed something to take up her time while Frank was away on his frequent road trips. At one point she had ninety-eight rose bushes before she took up another hobby: ceramics.

Ceramics quickly grew from a hobby to a major wholesale business, with three kilns in her backyard workshop supplying thirteen retail stores. This, in turn, led indirectly to her involvement with country music. In fact, this hobby helped her meet some of the country stars she idolized. When a star played in or around Charlotte she would make an ashtray with the star's name on it and use it to get backstage and introduce herself.

Lib frequented a beauty shop where "everybody loved John Harper," the country music disc jockey on WSOC. There was a strong rumor that Harper was getting canned, so Lib, in an effort to do something for him, organized a fan club—without ever asking him. On her own she enrolled a number of members and made John Harper ashtrays, impressing both Harper and the staff at WSOC.

Busy promoting John Harper, she met Loretta Lynn and Dottie West when they came to town, and convinced them to become members of Harper's fan club. This was another ticket to meet country stars and be involved in country music, and she took advantage of it.

Eventually the radio station asked her if she'd be interested in selling some advertising for the Saturday evening bluegrass show. While on her rounds she stopped at a local nightclub, Country City USA, to sell an ad promoting the appearance of singer Gene Watson. Later, she returned when the club was in full swing, and thought it had a lot of potential. It didn't matter that she had never had a drink of liquor, smoked a cigarette, or drank a cup of coffee (and still hasn't)—this was what she wanted to do.

The reason was fairly simple. She wanted to be in business for herself, knew about the restaurant business from her Kernersville days, and knew that clubs could book top country stars. It did not hurt that Gene Watson—one of her favorites, and one of the premier honky-tonk singers—was performing when she made that decision.

She bought an interest in the club in late 1976 and a couple of months later bought out partner Bill Jordan. She tried to interest John Harper in owning part of the club, but he was not interested. Then she cleaned up the place, redecorated, began promotions like serving free hors d'oeuvres, pizza, and hot dogs, and hired Harper to announce at the club three nights a week.

In February 1977 she began the eight-week series of talent contests that brought young Randy Traywick into the club.

Lib became determined that Randy Traywick could be a big country music star after hearing him sing during the talent contest. She was equally determined that she should play a major role, doing all she could, to make that dream come true. First, she put her foot down with Randy—letting him know some do's and don't's. Then she gave him lots of her time, letting him come out of his shell and talk.

When her husband told her to get rid of the club and send young Traywick back to Marshville, it was really not much of a choice. Frank Hatcher made his ultimatum as he was leaving for a road trip, and Lib insists that she began packing before the taillights were out of sight. Bags packed, she and Randy moved to another mobile home in the same development and set up housekeeping. By March 1980 the divorce was final and the property settled.

For the next six years, Lib would have Country City USA, which she moved to a bigger place down the road in May 1980, and Randy would sing six and seven nights a week for the folks who came.

Sometimes Harold Traywick would come to hear him. The problem with Harold's coming was that he never could behave himself. One friend from Marshville who accompanied Harold and Bobbie Rose one night to the club remembers Harold getting drunk, throwing bottles, and upsetting tables. Others remember him yelling threats and brandishing a gun—he almost always has a trusty .38 on him or nearby.

A family friend from Marshville remembers that "Randy was playing a lot and getting better and better. But Harold would get drunk and cause problems, and so Lib Hatcher didn't want him in the club."

The final straw came one night when Harold and Randy got into a serious argument out in the parking lot. It might have gotten nasty if Lib's bouncer, a huge man, had not been hovering in the background. Harold got frustrated, jumped in his car, and drove it into the side of the club. "That's right, drove it right inside. Knocked down the wall and everything."

With this act, Lib banned Harold from the club.

There was a major conflict over Randy between the ambitious, determined Lib Hatcher and the fiery, explosive Harold Traywick. Neither one liked to be told what to do, and both thought they knew best what to do for Randy. Lib didn't want Randy to go back to Marshville and hang out with his old running buddies, while Harold demanded Randy come home more often and show he had a greater allegiance to him than to Lib.

Randy was caught in the middle. He loved his daddy but knew him well; he knew there was no future staying in Marshville. And he trusted Lib Hatcher as he had never trusted anyone else before; something told him that here was where he belonged. That didn't make things any smoother, but at least there seemed to be some hope.

CHAPTER 7

*T*here's no smell worse than stale beer and hungover cigarette smoke. That's what a nightclub smells like in the
morning—as bad as a skunk on a country road. Those nightclub smells filled Lib Hatcher's nostrils for years.

Lib worked hard at her club, and it succeeded. There
were problems and conflicts, like the ones with Country
City USA's band, George Stoner and the Stonemen. Stoner
and his group were good, but did not have the fire in the
belly needed for success—they were satisfied with being
small-time heroes and big-time zeroes. But still there was
jealousy when Randy began singing with the group, especially when his name got top billing on the marquee.

In 1980 Lib sold the 250-seat club and bought a 400-seat
club with a motel next door and shop space to sell records,
western wear, and her ceramics. She took advantage of the
Urban Cowboy craze by buying a mechanical bull and driving to Texas to pick it up. That bull made so much money

shaking off Carolina cowboys that Lib was eventually to collect enough spending change to move to Nashville.

In an effort to promote Randy as a country singer, Lib began booking country stars from Nashville each month, although it was not financially profitable. But she wanted to make contacts, to have Nashville stars hear Randy sing, and this was the only way she knew how to do it. She also began meeting people involved in the music industry, people who would come to the club when one of the stars was performing.

Lib convinced one artist she had booked a number of times, Joe Stampley, to produce a session for Randy in Nashville, a session financed by Lib. It would cost Lib ten thousand dollars for the session and for the promotion and distribution promised by the Shreveport-based Paula Records.

Stampley produced two singles, "She's My Woman" and "I'll Take Any Willing Woman," the latter backed with "Dreamin'." When the singles were released, Lib and Randy hopped in their car and drove around the South to promote them on radio stations. The result was that one single, "She's My Woman," entered *Billboard*'s country charts on January 6, 1979, and stayed for four weeks, peaking at number ninety-one before falling off. The song, written by Jerry and Van Tassel, is an up-tempo number that begins with a funky, chicken-pickin' guitar riff. The vocal sounds much like Merle Haggard, and the melody in spots is reminiscent of the Beatles' "She's a Woman." The singer proclaims he loves his woman "like a bird loves a bug and a cat loves sweet milk." It's a nice start, but nothing to make a star.

Lib had John Harper play some tapes Randy made on his radio show. She had people writing songs for him, but the songs weren't quite up to snuff by Nashville standards. She also put together a top-notch band to play behind Randy at the club. And though she was trying to get some attention from Nashville, she was overwhelmed by lack of interest. Still, Lib and Randy were learning valuable lessons, although they were paying dearly for some of them. They were also meeting people who would help them further down the line. One person was Stan Byrd, national promotion director for Warner Brothers Records, who first came to the club when Lib booked Con Hunley.

Word had gotten around Nashville that Country City USA was the happening place in Charlotte—in fact, the only club booking country talent. If an artist wanted to play the Charlotte market, but could not draw enough to fill the Coliseum or get on a package show, then Lib's club was the only game in town.

Ann Tant was another person Lib met around this time. Ann was also working for Warner Brothers Records, living in Atlanta, and doing promotion. Ann's mother, "Mama Wynette," owned some clubs in Atlanta where country artists played, and Ann got Randy some bookings there.

Lib and Ann hit it off and became close friends. Both were eat up with Hillbilly Fever: the overwhelming, unquenchable, overpowering, undeniable, insatiable, overt love of country music and country music stars. This was the spark for their friendship and the flame that kept it going.

Lib and Randy talked a lot and became closer. Randy says that "for some reason, I would listen to Lib. She was a lot of guidance as far as just personal life and the music business. A combination between her and the music helped me straighten out—that and going to court and the judge telling me the next time I come, to bring my tooth brush."

Back in Marshville, the judge had made Randy go to counseling sessions. When the counselor asked him why he did things like raising hell and getting into so much trouble, Randy would get mad and have no answer. The problem was that Randy had never analyzed what he did or why he

31

did it; he had a tendency to react to whatever was going on at the time. He couldn't articulate his feelings and motives because he didn't understand them himself. Nor did he feel it was worth the effort to try.

Lib allowed Randy to develop more slowly, in a less threatening manner. She let him know she cared about him, and gradually he revealed himself to her—as well as to himself. With those revelations came the realizations that he did not *have* to get drunk and raise hell and tear things up. There were other things he could do with his time and other people's property. Simply put, Randy became exposed to another way of life.

One thing Lib did not do was put her foot down with Randy, setting boundaries and treating him like a wayward son, imposing discipline and letting him know there were things she would not tolerate. If you told Randy Traywick not to do something, that was exactly what he would do. If you laid down laws, he was sure to break them. Randy was a hardheaded kid who couldn't stand being told what to do. So Lib didn't give him orders; instead she listened to him.

Lib somehow saw the good in Randy that everyone else saw later but few could see then. She also saw a future country music star and shared that vision with Randy. He said later, "I don't remember exactly how she put it, but soon after she hired me at the club she asked me if I had ever thought about taking music seriously—and if I had, that she'd like to manage me and see what we could do with it. Nobody had ever really said that to me before."

Nobody had ever said it as often, either. Lib wanted to know where she stood: if Randy wasn't interested in striking it large in country music, he could go off and do as he pleased. But he would not be taking up any more of Lib's time and attention. Gradually, he began to see that he could be part of the country music world outside the confines of a North Carolina honky-tonk. That realization—that he wasn't just another dead-end kid—was startling in itself.

Lib Hatcher had one abiding passion in life: country music. When she met Randy and heard him sing she developed another passion: the career of young Randy Traywick. The two passions were linked—they were the same, really. Because she was so dedicated to country music, she became dedicated to Randy and his future. And being so dedicated to Randy's career meant she was dedicated to country music. At last she had found her mission in life, and she would spend her boundless energy fulfilling that calling.

Randy Traywick was being transformed, but it was not happening overnight. John Harper remembers the young, unfocused teenager during those first months at Country City USA. "At the time, he would rather shoot pool than sing," says Harper. "He absolutely loved to shoot pool. There was a pool table in the front of the club, and the stage was in the back. Many times I would introduce him, and he'd still be at the pool table."

The Charlotte years were critical to young Randy because he grew as a person as well as a performer. He learned to tame and control his personal life, and he learned how to be a performer. Playing six and seven nights a week at the club gave him a vast repertoire of songs, the self-confidence to get on a stage in front of people, and invaluable knowledge of what songs worked best for him as he developed a rapport with audiences.

This constant exposure to music and audiences is something every performer needs but few receive. Randy loved Hank Williams and wanted somehow to be like him. Ironically, there were a lot of similarities during these early years. Both Hank and Randy had strong women behind them. Hank's mother and then his wife Audrey pushed and encouraged Hank, while Lib filled that function for Randy. Hank had exposure on live radio shows—the principal way for country performers to get exposure during his time— while Randy had exposure in a club, the best way to receive it during his time.

Hank and Randy both started young. Hank was twelve when he began playing, Randy fourteen. Each knew from an early age he wanted to sing country music for the rest of his life.

But there were some important differences as well. Both Hank and Randy had a weakness for liquor and drugs; Randy would conquer his weakness and rise above it, but Hank never did. And that's where the biggest difference of all lies: Randy would live to see his thirtieth birthday; Hank never would.

CHAPTER 8

S ome say Charlotte could have been Music City USA instead of Nashville. Actually, a number of cities could have had that title: Atlanta, Knoxville, Memphis, Hollywood, Dallas, Charlotte, and others. Indeed, there wasn't much recording done in Nashville during the 1920s, when the major record labels first discovered country music.

The first country hit was recorded in Atlanta, Georgia, in 1923 by Fiddlin' John Carson for Okeh Records. The person in charge of the recording, Ralph Peer, recorded Fiddlin' John because Okeh's distributor and Atlanta record dealer Polk Brockman insisted there was a market. And since Okeh wanted to keep their distributor happy, they recorded Fiddlin' John singing and fiddlin' "The Little Old Log Cabin in the Lane" and "The Old Hen Cackled and the Rooster's Going to Crow."

When the New York executives heard the recording, they concluded it was "pluperfect awful," but held their noses, covered their ears, and kept their promise to Brockman by releasing it. Sales were brisk, and suddenly the strains of hill- billies singing and playing sounded sweet to those New Yorkers' ears.

Ralph Peer was one of those most responsible for many of the earliest recordings of hillbilly and blues music. He would load up recording equipment in his car or ship it by train to a city, take out some newspaper ads, and wait until local performers showed up to record.

Meanwhile, country musicians were hearing about these newfangled recordings and itching to get their music on them. It was easier than working on the farm or in a factory, so they clamored to get in.

Charlotte was an ideal location for field recording. By 1930 it was the largest city in the Carolinas, it was centrally located in the mill region, and it was the focal point for a web of highways, enhanced by the "Good Roads" program of Governor (and Charlotte resident) Cameron Morrison in the 1920s.

The first recording to take place in Charlotte was done by Ralph Peer for RCA Victor on August 9, 1927. Those ses- sions were part of the same tour of the South that resulted in Peer's discovery and recording of the Carter Family and Jimmie Rodgers in Bristol, Tennessee. No stars of that mag- nitude appeared in Charlotte on the forty-six sides recorded by Peer, who had by this time been lured to Victor from Okeh.

RCA Victor made the most recordings in Charlotte, fol- lowed by Decca. Among those who recorded in Charlotte from 1927 to 1945 were the Carter Family, Bill Monroe, Uncle Dave Macon, Roy Acuff, the Delmore Brothers, DeW- itt "Snuffy" Jenkins (whose three-finger style of banjo pick- ing became known as the "Scruggs style" after North Carolina native Earl Scruggs popularized it with Bill Monroe's Bluegrass Boys), the Briarhoppers, and the string- bands of the Mainer family.

Country radio began in Charlotte in 1922 on WBT, only two years after the introduction of commercial radio in the United States. Beginning as a 100-watt station, WBT increased its wattage first to 25,000 watts and by 1933 to 50,000, although its lack of clear channel status caused gaps in its coverage. In the later 1920s it became a CBS affiliate, the key station in the regional Dixie Network.

Two firms that were instrumental in their sponsorship of country music radio programs were Chicago's Consolidated Drug Trade Products Company and the Crazy Water Crystals Company, a laxative manufacturer headquartered in Mineral Wells, Texas.

Crazy Water Crystals had an office in Charlotte that recruited such acts as Dick Hartman's Tennessee Ramblers and Mainer's Mountaineers. The first Crazy Water Crystals program began in 1933 with the recurring announcement that "for fifty-six years, Crazy Water has come to the aid of the weak and the ailing, and it has made of them men and women ready to face life's hardships." In the late 1930s WBT's Crazy Barn Dance began.

Consolidated Drug Trade Products instigated the Briarhoppers program, "Briarhopper Time." At the same time, WSM's Grand Ole Opry and Chicago's National Barn Dance were both aired over the NBC network.

Charles Crutchfield, the Briarhoppers' announcer, became known for injecting parody into the program's broad rube comedy. "Crutch" would poke fun at Radio Girl perfume, Dolorbak hair dye, and Zymole Trokey's cough drops—all part of the Drug Trade line of products. But he saved his best comments for Peruna, an "all-purpose tonic" with a high alcohol content. Crutch would announce, "We don't care what you do with it. Put it in the radiator of your car— it'll clean it out." Fans could receive a picture of the band for a "Pee-roo-nee" boxtop. As a result of the successful promotion of Peruna, the Briarhoppers became one of the best-known groups in the area, while many people in the Piedmont Carolinas walked around with half a buzz most of the time.

In 1936 RCA Victor cut a number of sides in Charlotte. The recording equipment was set up in temporary studios in warehouse space on the top two floors of a three-story building at 208 South Tyron Street. The building belonged to Southern Radio Corporation, RCA's Carolina distributor of radios, recordings, and record players. Among those recording during this two-week period were the Carter Family and Jimmie Davis, later governor of Louisiana.

A rift with the Charlotte musicians' union, which objected to country musicians recording for twenty-five or fifty dollars a side, caused RCA later to shift their operations about thirty-five miles down the road, just over the state line, to Rock Hill, South Carolina. These sessions were held in the Andrew Jackson Hotel on Main Street in September 1938. Prior to this, in 1937 and 1938, RCA Victor had recorded in rooms on the top floor of the ten-story Hotel Charlotte at West Trade and Poplar Streets.

The Jefferson-Standard Life Insurance Company purchased WBT in 1945 and continued the Briarhopper show for a while. But the firm was not wedded to country music, and the radio shows ended. Crazy Water Crystals and Consolidated Drug Trade Products also cut back on their radio advertising after World War II as discount drugstore chains took over their markets. Too, in the 1950s radio received less advertising revenue because of the development of television, records replaced live talent on radio, and changing popular tastes made rock and roll the dominant music on the airwaves.

Though RCA's last important session in Charlotte occurred in 1949 and Capitol did a session there in the same year, major labels after World War II began increasingly to use studios rather than take field equipment to places such as Charlotte. And Nashville, with its permanent studios, became the chief place to record.

CHAPTER 9

*I*n late August 1981 Lib Hatcher bought a house at 1610 Sixteenth Avenue South, at the far end of Music Row. Lib admits that when she looked at it, the place "was so full of fleas that the real-estate lady didn't want to walk in here."

Soon after Randy and Lib set about fixing up the place they rented out offices to songwriter Keith Stegall, publicist Bonnie Rasmussen, and independent promotion man Stan Byrd the former national promotion director of Warner Brothers Records. This much-needed income helped pay for the house. Meanwhile, Randy and Lib lived upstairs in an apartment on the second floor.

They had been making trips to Nashville trying to interest Music Row since 1977, when they had signed their first manager/artist contract. That was the year Lib had secured a booking on Ralph Emery's early-morning local TV show.

It had been Randy's first trip to Nashville, his first time to see the Grand Ole Opry, and the first time he'd ever been that far from the Charlotte-Marshville area. On that first trip Randy was awed by the huge mountains. Lib remembers driving while Randy hung his head out the side window or pressed his forehead against the front windshield, staring open-mouthed at the Blue Ridge and Great Smokies. These mountains would have been even more awe inspiring to him if he could have seen them as they were one hundred million years ago, four or five times as high as they are now.

In the next few years both had come to realize they could not stay in Charlotte and have the kind of country music career Lib was aiming for. Lib had given it a good shot, though. Still, by the end of 1981 they were ready to take the next big step, establishing a base in Nashville. Lib had hired Pat Banks and her brother to run Country City USA while they were in Nashville during the week.

Thus began a period when Randy and Lib were keeping their ties in both Charlotte and Nashville. They would spend Friday, Saturday, and Sunday in Charlotte, playing at Country City USA, then in the early hours of Monday morning hop into their car and get over to I-85 heading south to Spartanburg, South Carolina. Here they would connect with I-26, heading northwest through the beautiful Blue Ridge Mountains, past the exit for Carl Sandburg's home, and on to Asheville, where they would hit I-40 heading west.

I-40 would carry them through the majestic Smoky Mountains, over the Pigeon River, and through the Cherokee National Forest. As the morning light was starting to break, they would see the rock formations where the road was cut through the mountains. These cuts show rock at the bottom without fossils, created more than five hundred million years ago when this area was covered by a shallow sea. A bit higher are rocks laid down three hundred million years ago in the Paleozoic era, when the earth's first forests began to grow.

The tops of these mountains are not sharp and saw-toothed like the Alps and Rockies; they were never overrun by glaciers when those ice sheets flowed down over North America during the Pleistocene age, a million years ago. These mountains became havens for plants and animals that were driven south when the glaciers pushed down from the North. The hardwood forests here are like those which once covered almost the whole earth.

At the North Carolina-Tennessee border, about 240 miles from Nashville, Lib and Randy would push on. If the clouds were low, the tops of the Smokies would be shrouded in a dull gray mist. Perhaps there would be a hawk, wings out-stretched, floating in a large, lazy circle between two mountains.

Off the road, they could look over and see rural farm-houses, each with a satellite dish in the yard nearby. On the radio, Alabama was dominating country music. Cowboy boots and hats were the things to wear, pickup trucks were the things to drive, country music was the thing to listen to.

About four hundred crisscrossed miles and seven hours later they would arrive in Nashville. It had been a frustrating time for Lib and Randy. On one hand, they knew they needed to be in Nashville—and were thrilled to be where the action was. On the other hand, it was a series of small encouragements and big rejections.

Lib and Randy had met Charlie Monk and Keith Stegall at the Acuff-Rose golf tournament earlier in 1981. They had been introduced by Ann Tant, and Randy sang some songs with his guitar while they were sitting around a hotel room. Also in the room was Gary Morris and some others milling about.

Charlie Monk was then head of CBS's publishing company in Nashville. He invited Lib and Randy to come by and play him some songs. Keith Stegall was impressed by Randy's talent and also encouraged him to come by. Never one to miss an opportunity to get a foot in the door, Lib quickly followed up. Soon she and Randy were frequenting the CBS offices, talking with Monk, wanting to convince him of Randy's talent and future.

Monk was most impressed with the song "I Told You So" because he thought it would be a natural for Lee Greenwood. Monk took this song, signed it to a publishing deal, and pitched it to Greenwood, who turned it down.

In 1982 Charlie left CBS and began his own publishing company. Lib and Randy continued to meet with Monk, who would pitch Randy's songs around town. They decided to have a contractual agreement, so attorney David Maddox drew up a copublishing agreement where Monk would have half of the publishing rights for Randy's songs and Lib would have the other half.

In pitching the songs for other artists to record, Charlie played them for a number of producers. Virtually no one was interested in either the singer or the songs—too country. And they just didn't hear any great talent there.

At this time, Monk was managing Keith Stegall, who had penned "Sexy Eyes" for Dr. Hook, "We're in This Love Together" for Al Jarreau, "Lonely Nights" for Mickey Gilley, and "Hurricane" for Leon Everette, among others. Though his energies and attention were centered on Stegall, Monk still wanted to develop a strong publishing company.

Keith had been most impressed with Randy as a songwriter. There was a depth to his songs, but at the same time most of the ideas seemed to be unfinished, not quite carried through to completion. Like others Randy was meeting at this time, Keith thought Randy showed an incredible talent and potential for songwriting. Nobody thought much about him as a singer.

Lib looked at Monk as a source of contacts as well as a source of help in management. She needed all the help she could get to launch Randy's career. She didn't feel she could pull off a major deal because she didn't know enough people; Monk did, but his hands were full trying to launch Stegall's career.

After the Paula singles, which cost Lib ten thousand dollars, she was more careful with her investments. She and Randy signed a six-month contract with producer John Ragsdale. He cut several songs—including "Promises"—but, although Curb Records showed some interest, in the end everybody turned them down. Since the extension of the contract depended upon Ragsdale getting a record deal, and since none was forthcoming, he released Randy and Lib and bid them good luck.

At Monk's publishing company, Keith took Randy into the studio several times to sing on demos—demonstration records to showcase songs for producers. Randy recorded a number of Keith's songs as well as some of his own. A lot of producers and label executives heard these songs, but everybody took an El Paso Pasadena, saying, "No thanks, Omaha, thanks a lot."

 CHAPTER *10*

*T*he year Randy moved to Nashville—1981—was the year of Alabama, who had two Gold Albums and two number-one singles. Other top artists were Willie Nelson, Roseanne Cash, T. G. Sheppard, Mickey Gilley, Conway Twitty, Ronnie Milsap, Hank Williams, Jr., and Charlie Pride.

Gold Albums—representing sales—were also awarded to George Jones, Loretta Lynn, Barbara Mandrell, Ronnie Milsap, Willie Nelson, Anne Murray, the Oak Ridge Boys, Dolly Parton, Eddie Rabbitt, Kenny Rogers, the Statler Brothers, Emmylou Harris, Conway Twitty, Conway and Loretta, Hank Williams, Jr., Larry Gatlin, Waylon Jennings and Jessie Colter, and such quasi-country acts as John Denver, Mac Davis, the Charlie Daniels Band, Juice Newton, and the Eagles.

It was a boom time for country music, still reaping the benefits from the previous year's *Urban Cowboy* craze, although the rest of the music industry was suffering a depression.

In that first year of Ronald Reagan's presidency, unemployment was 11 percent, the interest rates were zooming to over 20 percent, and the country was in a bad way. People with small businesses—like Lib's Country City USA club—were suffering from this economic plunge.

It was the year Gold Record awards for singles went to "Elvira" by the Oaks, "Nine to Five" by Dolly Parton, and two by Eddie Rabbitt—"I Love a Rainy Night" and "Drivin' My Life Away."

Plans were being laid for the creation of a cable network consisting of country programming. This network, to be financed by radio and television station WSM and its parent company, American General, would be headquartered at the Opryland complex, where Opryland amusement park and the Grand Ole Opry House were located, off Briley Parkway about fifteen miles east of Music Row.

After much planning and staffing, The Nashville Network (TNN) went on the air in April 1983.

As the Opryland complex had grown, shops, motels, and restaurants had sprung up in the area, taking advantage of the flow of tourists attracted to Opryland. And so it was that the Nashville Palace had been built in 1974 by John Hobbs. During the first year, it was known as "Jerry Reed's Nashville Palace," with Reed's name being used to draw fans. Reed never actually owned any of the club, but he appeared there a number of times that first year.

In September 1982 Lib began working at the Nashville Palace. She needed a job in Nashville, but she also needed a base of operations, and she could hardly do better than the Palace, located less than a mile from the Grand Ole Opry House and the Nashville Network. Opry stars and Nashville Network executives would stop by often, and the club welcomed big names to its tables and stage.

Lib had been hired by John Hobbs after being recommended by Opry star Ray Pillow. She went out to the club and met with Hobbs, who was impressed by her credentials and, on the basis of Pillow's recommendation, hired her. The next morning she was working there.

Lib was efficient and effective and set about making the Palace a top club and restaurant. She soon hired Randy as a dishwasher for two hundred dollars a week. By January 1983 she had him performing regularly on stage with the band.

Randy had been out to the Palace before, especially on Monday and Tuesday nights, when there was an open mike for songwriters. Here he got his first exposure to the song-writer audiences who sat quietly and listened to his songs. This came as quite a surprise to a singer who had been used to competing with the noise of partying honky-tonkers who considered the singer part of the background atmosphere and ambience. This new, passive audience stunned Randy— he thought at first they didn't like him.

These years at the Nashville Palace were tough for Lib and for Randy, whose work in the hot, busy kitchen was no pic-nic under any conditions. John Hobbs, a demanding, over-bearing, and hard-driving businessman, was especially rough on Lib, treating her brusquely and rudely at times.

Randy is mild-mannered and easygoing, but sometimes his anger would near the boiling point, just below the surface, and he would drop his head to the side—a mannerism to cover his shyness—and shake it slowly side to side with his chin nearly touching his shoulder as his fists would double. On more than one occasion he wanted to take John Hobbs out into the parking lot and beat the hell out of him; on more than one occasion he came awful close.

On the other hand, there was some genuine warmth be-tween Hobbs and his two employees. At times Hobbs could be kind, giving, and generous with them, extending them a helping hand in numerous ways. During those times Hobbs was more than a boss—he was a generous patron.

But the bottom line was that Randy needed the job and

needed the Palace, and so he listened to Lib, who convinced him to put up with the crap a little longer. She pushed him toward the stage, although he didn't need much prodding. Soon he was singing with the house band whenever he could. Hobbs would give him an extra fifty dollars a week for performing. His name was changed to Randy Ray, a result of the frustrations of trying to have people remember *Traywick* and some brainstorming by Lib and Ann Tant.

Randy and Lib worked evenings at the Palace, which meant they would go into work about 4:00 P.M. Randy would work in the kitchen until nine, then go on stage and sing. During the tourist season the hours were almost endless. They would go to work at 5:00 A.M. and work till the wee hours during these busy times.

Lib remembers one night when the band introduced Randy while he was in the middle of turning steaks. He looked at her desperately, and said, "What'm I gonna do?" She said, "Go sing, I'll turn 'em."

Those who worked for Lib during this time remember her as likeable but demanding. She always made sure they had something to do and kept pushing them to stay as busy as she was. Those waitresses also remember Lib being absolutely dedicated to—some say fanatical about and consumed with—making Randy Travis a star. She would make sure there was a coat in the kitchen for him to slip on when he shed his white apron and stepped out to perform.

The waitresses also remember Lib keeping a close eye on young Randy. They would make bets among themselves about how long it would take Lib to arrive on the scene if Randy began talking with another girl. For some reason conversations between Randy and young females never lasted long around the Palace. Lib always insisted she was looking out for Randy's best interests, making sure he was unencumbered in his pursuit of country music stardom instead of being derailed and distracted by the kinds of girls who hung out in bars.

 **CHAPTER 11**

𝒯he house Lib bought in 1981 sits just off Sixteenth Avenue, a street that used to be the driveway connecting West End Avenue and Belmont Mansion. When its first owner, Mrs. Adelicia Aklen, moved into the mansion in 1850, the area beside the driveway was filled with trees, flowers, and open field.

Less than a hundred yards to the south of the house is Wedgewood Avenue, and about a mile to the west is Hillsboro Avenue. At the corner of Hillsboro and Wedgewood sits the old Hillsboro Theater, a movie house that used to be the home of the Grand Ole Opry in the 1930s. Today it houses the Educator's Credit Union.

Down Hillsboro Road going toward Green Hills, about a block away on a small side street, is the Tennessee Book Company, former home to one of the first studios Harold and Owen Bradley built in Nashville.

People trace country music in Nashville back to the

Grand Ole Opry, begun by WSM in 1925, but it didn't become big business there until 1943, when Roy Acuff put up
twenty-five thousand dollars and he and Fred Rose became
partners in the Acuff-Rose Publishing Company. They were
soon followed by such other publishing companies as Hill
and Range, Tree, Cedarwood, and Pamper. In 1947 Acuff-
Rose signed a young Alabama songwriter named Hank Williams.

For a long time the music business was located downtown along Broadway. On Fifth Avenue was the Ryman Auditorium, then home of the Grand Ole Opry. A side door
opened onto an alley leading to Tootsie's, a bar the Opry
members frequented between sets. Across Broadway was
the Ernest Tubb Record Shop, where the Midnight Jamboree
was held after the Opry performances concluded.

WSM was situated in the National Accident and Life Insurance Building on Union, where the National General Building is now located. In a makeshift studio in that building
Eddy Arnold recorded for Victor in 1944; that was the first
recording session in Nashville.

Across the street sat the old Tulane Hotel, where a suite
held Castle Studios, the first real studio in Nashville. At this
site, where the Nashville Public Library now sits, three WSM
engineers, George Reynolds, Carl Jenkins, and Aaron Shelton, inaugurated their studio by recording a jingle for
Shyer's Jewelers.

On that session were singer Snooky Lanson, who later
achieved fame as one of the singers on "Your Hit Parade,"
Owen Bradley on piano, Harold Bradley on guitar, and
George Cooper on bass. Owen Bradley later became one of
the most famous producers in Nashville, helping create the
"Nashville Sound" of Patsy Cline, Ernest Tubb, Kitty Wells,
Loretta Lynn, and other country legends. Harold became the
godfather of the session guitar players (he still does sessions
today), while Cooper, who was then head of the Nashville

branch of the American Federation of Musicians, was responsible for one of the most significant but unheralded acts for the country music industry.

It was Cooper who convinced the American Federation of Musicians to suspend their rule requiring applicants to pass a test of musical literacy—reading and writing sheet music—in order to join the union. That allowed instrumentalists who played by ear—most of the early musicians in country music—to get paid scale and thus make a living. Nashville was thus able to develop as a recording center, with talented musicians, playing by ear, providing musical backup and creating the Nashville Sound as well as the Nashville method of "head sessions" (improvising in the studio) that has been a cornerstone of country music recording.

Nashville—unlike the other music centers, New York and Los Angeles—has its music industry centralized on Music Row. The first music business on the Row was the Bradley Film and Recording Studio, set up by Owen and Harold Bradley in 1955 on property they purchased for about seventy-five hundred dollars. They chose that area because it had just been zoned for commercial use, having previously been a residential neighborhood since the 1920s, when houses were built in what used to be Mrs. Acklen's fields and gardens. The property was cheap. This studio became an Army-surplus Quonset hut, around which the current CBS Records office building now sits at 34 Music Square East.

In 1956 RCA leased a building on Seventeenth Avenue to use as a recording studio, and Cedarwood Publishing, built by the Denny family on Sixteenth Avenue South, became the first music office building on the Row. During the 1960s other music firms began moving from downtown out to this growing Music Row.

The Country Music Association was formed in 1958, the

same year two other important music organizations started up—the National Association of Recording Arts and Sciences, which presents the Grammys, and the Recording Industry Association of America, which certifies Gold and Platinum Albums. Although it is not popular to admit this now, these organizations were all formed, in part, as a backlash against rock and roll. Industry leaders felt compelled to try to save the music business from the wild, young upstarts in the rock revolution.

In 1961 the Country Music Hall of Fame, patterned after the Baseball Hall of Fame in Cooperstown, New York, was inaugurated with the induction of Hank Williams, Fred Rose, and Jimmie Rodgers. In 1967 the Country Music Hall of Fame building, situated at the head of Music Row, was opened. By the 1970s most of the major structures that define Music Row were in place, and portions of the old streets were renamed Music Square East and West, Music Circle South and North, Roy Acuff Place, and Music Alley.

For a long time, companies took over old houses along the Row and converted them into offices, giving them a more homey feel than their big-city counterparts. It was one of these old homes that Lib Hatcher bought and renovated, thus continuing a country music tradition that began over twenty years before. The house served as a focal point for Randy and Lib's life. Lib would cook lunches and dinners and invite people over, making contacts. She leased office space to *Radio and Records,* an industry trade publication, and to JoAnne Gardner, who later formed a video company with Roseanne Cash.

Lib invited to dinner people connected with the music industry—like Charlie Monk—people from the Opry and WSM, and anyone else she thought might help Randy's career. For these meals Lib would save her money, then go down to Farmer's Market in northern Nashville and load up on fresh vegetables and other goodies.

Songwriter Johnny Russell (he wrote "Act Naturally") became a regular visitor because he loved to eat. Ann Tant and her husband, Tiny, would stay there too; Ann sometimes stayed for weeks.

Ann and Lib were close friends at this time, like sisters, though they would have occasional spats and falling outs. Ann had lost her job in Atlanta at Warner Brothers when Jimmy Bowen took over the label. It was Bowen's policy to release almost everyone with a label when he was named head and then staff the company with people who were loyal to him. Some of those who had been working there before had been kept on; most hadn't. Ann was in the majority, so she was spending time in Nashville trying to pick up some accounts as an independent promotion person.

Randy would give tapes of his songs to Keith Stegall, who taught Randy some of the basics of the craft of songwriting. Randy says Keith showed him there are "certain directions a song needs to go in instead of wandering off everywhere." Keith was also keeping tabs on Randy's career and would go out to the Nashville Palace and listen to him.

Stan Byrd, whose independent promotion firm, Chart Attack, had offices in the house, would hire Randy to do yard work and work on his farm. Stan remembers him being the "hardest worker" he ever knew. Randy was never afraid of hard work; indeed, he seemed to enjoy good, strong physical labor.

Randy was also working out regularly, a hobby he had started back in 1977 in Charlotte when he bought his first small bench-press outfit. By 1982 Randy was going to a health club and "running the Row," covering the several-mile area from their house up to Division Street and the Country Music Hall of Fame and back.

Lib was the leader and organizer; Randy worked on the house when he wasn't at the Palace or making the rounds on Music Row. But there were some fights too, mostly over

Randy's wanting to see his family. Lib would insist he stay in Nashville; though they would argue loudly, Lib usually had her way. On one occasion, however, Randy just took off for Marshville for a few days. It was unlike him, but the tension was just too much.

It was then—January 1982—that he had his final brush with the law, getting arrested for DWI and put in the jail in Wadesboro, Anson County, just south of his parents' home in Peachland.

Some people think that becoming a star is a bit of magic. But it's a lot of hard work—methodical and persistent. It takes pulling together a press kit and a tape, making appointments and calls, working constantly.

Stardom is not one giant break, one sudden step, like being discovered in a drugstore. It is a series of small steps, meeting a lot of people whose interlocking relationships provide the key contacts, rather than meeting the one person who can do it all. Lib and Randy were making these small steps, meeting a variety of people who would help them further down the line. They didn't quite realize it then, but they were building a firm foundation for future stardom, inch by inch, brick by brick.

And while they knew that each brick and each little step was important, it was impossible to see the whole house yet, or even to know if they were building a mansion or just a shapeless pile of bricks.

 CHAPTER 12

*L*ib was always trying to get Randy more recognition and exposure. The Nashville Network, set to begin in April 1983, had planned a program for unknown talent hosted by Bill Anderson. On March 17, 1983, Randy auditioned for the show, "You Can Be a Star," in one of the trailers located behind the Opry House.

Sitting in a chair with his Gibson guitar, he looked at the camera and said, "My name is Randy Ray and I want to be a star." Then he sang two songs, "You Ain't Seen Nothing Yet" and "Ain't No Use." At the audition, Randy and Lib left two phone numbers where they could be reached—one at the Nashville Palace and the other at the Fiddler's Inn next door. The producers never called back. Instead, Lang Scott was the winner of the April star search, while Floyd Brown won in October.

Frustrated from her futile attempts to get a major label interested in Randy, Lib decided to do a custom album at the Nashville Palace. A "custom" album means one that is paid for and distributed by the singer or someone around him, as opposed to an album produced and distributed by an established label. Since no established label was interested in Randy, a custom record was the only way to get something out.

Lib knew that a lot of people came to the Palace and that selling the album would be easy. Tourists come into town with ready cash and are likely to buy an album of an artist they have just heard. They enlisted Keith Stegall as producer, and John Hobbs offered to put up the money—about forty-five hundred dollars. Hobbs had given Lib a choice: either she could have a Christmas bonus or he would finance Randy's album. Lib didn't have to deliberate long.

Originally, Lib was going to spend about two thousand dollars and record on a basic, two-track tape recorder. But Keith and others advised against it, saying the quality would be too poor and would not represent Randy well. Too, Johnny Rosen's sound truck—his mobile recording facilities—would not cost that much more, and the finished tape would be master quality.

John Hobbs knew Lib wanted the album badly and also thought it might be good advertising for the Palace. And so in November 1982 they recorded at the Palace.

Randy Ray Live at the Nashville Palace begins with Randy being introduced by Charlie Monk. The first song, "Ain't No Use," is a lively number with plenty of steel and a lead guitar that sounds a little like the Beatles' "I Feel Fine." Next is "If It Was Love That Kept You Here," a ballad, followed by another up-tempo number, "Free Rider," which Randy introduces as "for all the men we've got in the audience tonight." The intro to the song is reminiscent of Merle Haggard's "Workin' Man," and the lyrics yearn for a "pretty woman" who will "pay for having me around" because "I don't want to lay no money down."

A ballad about lost love, "You Ain't Seen Nothing Yet," and a Texas honky-tonk shuffle, "One Last Time," follow before side 1 closes with "Reasons I Cheat." This ballad deals with the frustrations and hopelessness of everyday life. The singer—aging, stuck in a dead-end job, his children growing, and his wife not understanding "why I stay dead on my feet"—attempts to explain and justify his succumbing to the smile of a willing woman. It could have been written with Conway Twitty in mind, with its crescendo of increasing emotion that pushes onward and upward as the vocal register climbs.

Side 2 begins with "Call Somebody Who Gives a Damn," and Randy thanks Mama Wynette in Atlanta—Ann Tant's mother—for the idea. This is followed by the honky-tonk ballad "I Told You So," then "Promises," with a full band. This song about trying to correct a wayward life and straighten a crooked path leads into "Send My Body Home on a Freight Train" with an up-tempo shuffle on the drums.

Randy introduces "Future Mister Me" as "kind of a true story—happened to a friend of mine." It's a ballad about checking out an old lover's new man to make sure she is in good hands.

In the final song, "Good Intentions," influences from a host of Merle Haggard's songs—"Branded Man," "Hungry Eyes," "Mama Tried," "Sing Me Back Home," and "Hickory Hollow's Tramp"—can all be heard. It is a "Mama" song, based on the proverb "The road to hell is paved with good intentions." It also displays the country songwriter's love of word play, giving a new twist to a familiar expression to find a "hook."

Lib had been working hard at the Palace, putting in lots of hours to make the club run smoothly and be a top drawing card for tourists coming to Nashville. In December, as the album was being mixed and overdubs added by Keith at Polyfox Studio—a small, inexpensive studio located beside

Owen Bradley's old Quonset hut—Lib came into the studio and listened. Maybe this would be the big break to launch Randy as a country star.

On the cover is a picture of Randy sitting at a table with amps and the Nashville Palace sign in back. He is wearing an open-necked shirt with silver studs on the tips of the big collar. There is a horseshoe-shaped diamond ring on one hand, a guitar-shaped diamond ring on the other. He has long hair and looks like a million other honky-tonk singers dreaming of stardom.

CHAPTER 13

It's hard to consider 1984 a high point for country music when one of the year's number-one songs on the country charts was "To All the Girls I've Loved Before" by Willie Nelson and Julio Iglesias, which won the duo a Country Music Association award. The CMA's top male vocalist was Lee Greenwood, the top song "Wind beneath My Wings," and the top single and album "A Little Good News" by Anne Murray. The top country artist on the *Billboard* singles chart in 1984 was Kenny Rogers, followed by Alabama, Earl Thomas Conley, Janie Fricke, Lee Greenwood, Mickey Gilley, Barbara Mandrell, Willie Nelson, John Anderson, and Michael Martin Murphey.

Clearly, this was not a good year for traditional country music.

Still, there were some rumblings of change as well. Merle Haggard had two number-one songs, the Judds hit with "Mama He's Crazy" and "Why Not Me," Ricky Skaggs had two number one's (including "Uncle Pen"), and Conway Twitty had three, as did George Strait—"Let's Fall to Pieces Together," "Does Fort Worth Ever Cross Your Mind," and "Right or Wrong." And at the end of the year the top country album was George Strait's *Right or Wrong* followed by Ricky Skaggs's *Don't Cheat in Our Home Town.* There were some real country songs and country artists out there, but their fans had to try hard to find them. Country radio was playing something else.

The problem came directly from Music Row itself. By the early 1980s Nashville was filled with executives who did not like country music. They had grown up in an urban environment on rock and roll, and that's where their hearts remained. The radios in their cars and offices were generally tuned to pop stations, and they openly disparaged the country audience.

Many were now armed with college degrees and a taste for the music biz. They liked the glitter and gleam more than they liked the music, and if it took Nashville and country music to put them at the edge of the spotlight, well, so be it. Many openly admitted they didn't like the earlier, traditional country music—the "whiny stuff" or "twang," as they called it—but liked the new acts who were actually rockers in cowboy shirts. They wanted to call the music something other than "country"—like "Americana" or "Nashville."

They did not realize a basic fact: country music *is* the whiny stuff, and country music fans were getting sick and tired of these pop acts and pop records coming out of Nashville under the guise of "country" music.

Country radio had arrived at a point where stations would not play acts or records they considered "too country," victims of consultants armed with demographic surveys and dollar signs who convinced them that if they watered down this stuff everybody would like it. Too, a large number of country radio programmers and disc jockeys didn't care much for real country music either—most had never even heard a Lefty Frizzell record, much less played one on the air. Advertisers wanted listeners and listeners wanted country, so the programmers played country. But in an effort to reach everybody they played a watered-down country stripped of its soul.

The executives on Music Row had convinced themselves and others of what they wanted to believe all along—that there was no market for "traditional" country music. Yes, it was part of the past, but there was definitely no future in it. Their world was just too hip for all that twang.

But the fact remained that there had always been a market for traditional country music and that this whiny sound—which in essence defines country music—was what country listeners wanted. This was a hard point to accept by the Music Row types because they simply didn't like this music and didn't want it around. And they figured that if they didn't like it, then nobody important liked it.

Thus they signed acts with little or no country heritage or even love for the music. As a matter of fact, the great majority of those "country" acts signed were more in love with stardom than they were with the music. The music and Nashville were just a vehicle to become a star. Their egos were in it even though their hearts weren't. And their minds weren't deep enough to know the difference.

Perhaps the problem could be traced back to Hank Williams himself, that quintessential country act, whose songs, interpreted by such pop singers as Tony Bennett and Rosemary Clooney, expanded the boundaries of country music. Then there was Eddy Arnold, who replaced Roy Acuff as the most widely known and most successful country singer in the late 1940s. While Arnold was at the pinnacle of country music stardom he dismissed his steel guitar player, Little Roy Wiggins, replaced him with strings and a pop sound, and traded his cowboy suit for a tuxedo in an effort to reach a more sophisticated urban audience.

The country artist—indeed, the rural southerner—has always yearned for acceptance and respectability. Country music was a way to break the bonds of poverty and anonymity. But once attained, the country performer wanted to be accepted and respected by the city folks who disdained his music. Hence he changed it, made it smoother.

The country executives, often led by the chamber of commerce for country music—the Country Music Association—saw anything that led to bigger markets, increased visibility, and more acceptance and respect from big-city types as "progress." Thus they prodded the artists to disparage their rural roots and become more citified. There was an element of frustration here, too. The older executives had seen poor southern boys and girls become country artists but keep their rural mentality. They thought small, unable to imagine the bigger world of show biz. They tended to limit themselves and cut short their own—as well as country music's—potential. Not comfortable living in a society they didn't know or trust, they preferred to live in their own little world. Convinced that the big awards and big money were far beyond them, they stuck with rhinestone suits and Cadillacs as their goals. But as a handful of artists found financial success by altering their musical style, more and more country musicians were won over.

Traditional country music was limited and watered down by country artists themselves as well as by the outsider executives. By the 1980s few country artists had any ambition to be a member of the Grand Ole Opry, and most executives in country music openly bragged about how much they avoided the Saturday night show that still packed 'em in. Indeed, this may seem hard to believe, but there are still a number of industry people on Music Row who have never even seen the Grand Ole Opry.

It is no wonder that a singer as unabashedly country as Randy Travis would find it difficult to get a major recording contract. It is also highly ironic that some singers and songs could be considered "too country" for country music—but that was the shape of things in the early 1980s when Randy Travis and Lib Hatcher were knocking on doors. They would go a long way toward changing that.

CHAPTER *14*

*N*ineteen eighty-four was a crucial year for Randy. It began with his first national television appearance on January 18, when he appeared on "Nashville Now" with Ralph Emery on the fledgling Nashville Network.

Along with Randy on the show were the Brower Brothers and Barbara Mandrell, who introduced "Randy Ray" to the audience. She announced he was a performer at the Nashville Palace and that he had recorded a live album there.

Performing in black pants and a gray western-cut sport coat, he was obviously nervous as he sang "Send My Body Home on a Freight Train." After the performance, Ralph Emery came over to chat with him and asked, "Why is this microphone shaking?" Randy laughed and said, "That's a good question," before admitting he was nervous. Ralph assured him. "Randy, don't be nervous. You're among friends."

At the end of the show, Randy joined the Brower Brothers, Mandrell, and Ralph singing "I'll Fly Away," with Barbara taking the lead and the rest joining on the chorus.

Randy made several other appearances on "Nashville Now" during the year. On July 16, when he sang "I Told You So," Emery introduced him as "the cook who became a singer," alluding to his stint as a short-order cook at the Nashville Palace.

Randy had sung "Ain't No Use" in the first half of the program, then came over and talked with Ralph as Emery showed the live album over the air. When Emery asked if he was still cooking, Randy replied, "Not as often."

Emery then asked why he took the job as a cook, and Randy replied that he "didn't have a job and had to make a living," adding that he "had never cooked before, but learned real quick."

Ralph noted that a lot of people move to Nashville and take any job just to get going, then told Randy, "I hope you will be a major force in country music."

"I hope so," said Randy. "We're working on it."

Randy next appeared on "Nashville Now" on September 19, when Johnny Russell sat in as host. Russell noted, as he introduced Randy Ray, that "we go to the movies a lot together, and we eat a lot together 'cause he's got a manager who can really cook."

Randy sang a song Johnny Russell had co-written (with Dickie Lee and Tommy Rocco) for George Straight called "Let's Fall to Pieces Together." After the song Randy admitted that "we get a lot of requests" for that song at the Palace.

On the show was another guest, legendary songwriter Tommy Collins. Randy said he had been writing songs with Tommy as well as with Keith Stegall.

Lib had been booking Randy onto some local Nashville shows as well. On July 6 and December 6 he appeared on the "Waking Crew," an early-morning radio show broadcast live on WSM from the Stage Door Lounge at the Opryland Hotel. He also appeared on "Channel Four Magazine," a local television show hosted by Charlie Chase.

Randy had gotten on Emery's national show for several reasons. First, the show was just beginning, and its producers were struggling to fill ninety minutes each night. They had not yet reached the position where all the major acts wanted and needed the show. Second, Lib had been very persistent with Debbie Brawner, who was in charge of booking the talent on "Nashville Now," convincing her to give Randy a shot on the show.

Finally, Randy was in a strategic position: he was performing less than a mile away, and Opry performers and others from TNN would regularly drop in at the Palace, where they could see and hear him. The TV crew and band had done "Nashville After Hours" on location at the Nashville Palace, and they had liked Randy personally and been impressed with his talent. They, too, had recommended him to Debbie Brawner.

The connection between Music Row and the Grand Ole Opry, though interesting, is not as close as most people think. Basically, Music Row is the power force in country music, controlling who gets recorded. It is on Music Row that the country music star-making machine grinds on full-time, generally oblivious to the Opry and its tradition.

The Opry, meanwhile, serves as a mecca for country music fans who come from all over the United States to see this legendary institution. The shows are packed—particularly in the summer—and the Opry performers are still stars to those who visit the Opry, even though the Music Row community virtually ignores most of them.

In the mid-1970s and 1980s most of the major stars in country music neglected the Opry, not joining and perhaps playing there only once or twice just to say they had done so. People on Music Row ignored the Opry because they felt it had nothing to do with contemporary country music; the folks who came to town were tourists, and the Opry was a local attraction, not really related to the country music they were marketing nationally.

There was even a little antagonism between the two. Opry performers often could no longer find a recording contract from a major label, and the recordings they did make—generally on small labels—were not played on the radio. The Opry had become a world of its own, an island in the country music community, with little if any influence on the records coming out of Music Row.

The Opry itself was partly to blame for this. In the early days it was the Opry and not Music Row that held the power. The publishing companies and recording studios were originally downtown near the Ryman Auditorium, home of the Opry, but gradually moved out to Sixteenth and Seventeenth Avenues South. The Opry did not need Music Row because the Opry dominated country music; where they led, Music Row would surely follow.

As is so often the case, those in power thought it would last forever, that things would never change. But things always do change, and whoever is on top is almost certain not to remain there unchallenged. As the balance of power in country music shifted to Music Row with its publishing and recording companies, talent agencies, and studios, they snubbed the Opry just as they themselves had been snubbed.

But by the mid-1980s it was Music Row's turn to feel the effects of arrogance and pride. As they ignored the Opry community, the music they called country drifted further and further away from the tradition established by the Opry, until the two sounds were almost at odds. Music Row thought the Opry was a thing of the past; they forgot that the show's tradition and heritage continues to define country music. And that tradition and heritage cannot be ignored if country music is to keep its identity.

Too, the Opry folks had to keep listening to country fans because this was their bread and butter: attracting tourists to Nashville and providing them with a memorable experience. It forced them to keep their ear close to the ground and remain aware of the tastes of these core fans. Music Row, on the other hand, was increasingly dominated by corporate giants. This meant they kept their ear on the phone to New York and Los Angeles and other folks inside the business. They were paying attention to their peers at the expense of the country fans, whose tastes and response got lost in the razzle-dazzle of high-roller show biz.

Ironically, it was the Nashville Network that caused Music Row to begin taking the Opryland complex seriously again and to make the fifteen-mile drive over to Briley Parkway. The network brought country music into living rooms with the medium that dominates American lives. And on the Nashville Network Ralph Emery, a former disc jockey at WSM, emerged as the biggest and brightest star. Before long, his show would be TNN's centerpiece. As the music took a turn back toward traditionalism and the heritage of the Opry, due to the increased television exposure provided by the Nashville Network, the Music Row power brokers once again had to deal with the Opryland network as a major force in country music.

Randy and Lib were in a unique position—part of both worlds. Randy was living on Music Row and performing at the Palace. Lib courted the Opry crowd at the same time she and Randy made regular forays to the offices on the Row.

Too, she made sure Randy was getting lots of local attention. On October 7, when *Amusement Business,* an industry magazine that reports on fairs, concerts, and other live attractions, held their annual party for those attending the International Country Music Buyers Association meetings, Randy and Lib were there meeting people. Randy performed at a showcase at Cajun's Wharf. He also emceed and performed at a fund-raiser for Albert Gore, Jr., who was leaving his seat in the House of Representatives to run for the Senate, and appeared on the cover of *Key* magazine, a local publication distributed to motel rooms informing tourists and travelers about local entertainment and restaurants.

At the end of November Randy and Lib attended the Fair Buyers convention in Las Vegas, meeting key bookers and promoters in an attempt to get some bookings at these events. On the songwriting front, Randy's song "I Told You So" was the B side of a single by Darrell Clanton on Warner Brothers.

Randy and Lib were both staying busy, working hard, making themselves known to the country music community. On one hand, they seemed to be sitting on the doorstep to country music stardom; but on the other hand, the door stayed locked.

CHAPTER 15

$\mathcal{I}$n November 1984 the Country Music Association conducted a series of seminars on marketing country music. A panel chaired by Mary Ann McCready discussed ways
to get market shares, attract young record buyers, and market records. A retailer commented, "My customers don't
think what they're getting is country music." One of those
listening was Martha Sharp of the A and R (artists and repertoire) department at Warner Brothers, the department in
charge of finding and signing new acts.

"It was like a light bulb went off," says Martha. "We'd
been shoving this stuff out and not listening to what people
were saying about it. A lot of people (in the record industry) thought traditional, hard-core country music was unac-
ceptable to young people and that to reach young people
you had to be more pop, more rock."

Martha began to think that "if you could find a young,
attractive—sexy, if you will—country music artist and cut

great records on him, what would happen? Let's just see what would happen!"

Warner Brothers was a relative newcomer to Music Row, having established an office there only in 1974. In November 1984—while Martha was listening to this panel discussion—Warner Brothers had a roster that included the Nitty Gritty Dirt Band, Johnny Lee, Eddie Rabbitt, John Anderson, Hank Williams, Jr., Crystal Gayle, Emmylou Harris, Conway Twitty, T. G. Sheppard, Gary Morris, Pam Tillis, Ray Price, Karen Brooks, and the duo of David Frizzell and Shelly West.

A number of these acts—such as Conway, Sheppard, Hank, Jr., and Crystal Gayle—had achieved success at other labels before signing with Warner Brothers. That means Warner Brothers had not "broken" them, a music-biz euphemism for taking them from being an unknown to a star.

Other artists—like Ray Price—had had their major successes elsewhere and were not repeating them at Warner Brothers. Still others had been around for a long while, and in order for a label to continue to succeed, it needs to find and develop new acts. The only two new acts on the label at this time were Karen Brooks and Pam Tillis.

This reflected a changing of the guard—and a corresponding change of philosophy—at Warner. Previously, when Jimmy Bowen—a legendary producer and executive—had headed the label, the prevailing philosophy was to sign big-name acts to big-time deals and get on the charts. But when Bowen left early in 1983 and Jim Ed Norman took the reins, the new philosophy was "Let's invest in the future: find new acts and build them."

Martha Sharp did not particularly care for country music. She had grown up on pop, rock, and classical music and later drifted toward folk music in the early 1960s when Peter, Paul, and Mary were dominating folkdom.

She had written some big songs in the 1960s: "Born a Woman" and "Single Girl" for Sandy Posey, each of which reached the number-twelve position on the pop charts in 1966, and "Come Back When You Grow Up" for Bobby Vee, which reached number three in 1968.

In the late 1970s Martha was working on a master's degree in human development counseling from Peabody College, located several blocks off Music Row. Martha asked her friend Dixie Gamble if her husband, Jimmy Bowen, then head of Elektra Records, was looking for any part-time help in the summer. That led to Martha filling in as a receptionist and then as an assistant to Bowen.

After Martha received her degree Bowen assigned her the job of screening songs for him. Since Bowen was a major producer, publishers and songwriters all over Music Row sent him songs; the job of the assistant was to listen to these tapes, reject those not suitable, and pass the good ones along to Bowen.

One day Bowen called her in and told her he was going to make her director of A and R. Martha swallowed hard and accepted; she was ready for a challenge.

Later, Elektra merged with Warner Brothers and Jimmy Bowen left for MCA, where he headed up that label. Martha stayed and eventually was named vice president of A and R.

The term "new traditionalism" had been cropping up in the music industry since Ricky Skaggs had burst onto the charts for CBS. Skaggs played traditional music, and fans loved it. Then George Strait was signed by MCA; he, too, played a traditional music that fans loved. Martha was not so much a visionary as an observant realist: she knew Warner Brothers needed their own Ricky or George, and so she set about looking for him.

After the CMA seminar Martha was having lunch with Judy Harris, who was with CBS publishing. She told Judy she was looking for a male traditional country singer, and Judy—a dyed-in-the-wool country fan—immediately suggested Randy Ray, mentioning that Charlie Monk was working with him. At a music-industry party at ASCAP Martha ran into Charlie Monk and asked him about Randy. Charlie replied that Keith Stegall was in the studio working on a tape for Randy at the time and that he would get a copy over to her.

Meanwhile, Lib was impatient to get more recognition for Randy. She was planning to put out a single and try for some airplay on country radio again. The single would be two songs Randy had cut as demos for Charlie and Keith. At the time she called Monk, Keith was in the studio mixing down the singles. Monk told her there would be a tape ready by four P.M. When Keith was finished in the studio, he dropped it by Warner's for Martha, who in the meantime had scheduled a visit to the Nashville Palace with Monk to see Randy perform.

On November 28 Charlie picked up first Keith and Diane Stegall, then Martha, and drove out to the Palace, where they had dinner and watched Randy perform. Randy knew Martha was coming and had been singing awhile before she got there. After his set, he and Lib met Martha at her table and chatted a while, then Martha left. Randy thought at the time, "Well, there goes another one," because he didn't believe she was interested.

Quite the opposite was true. Martha had thought, "Here is a kid who sings great and has got some songs. I'm really attracted to him; he's so shy and sweet and just a dear guy. His biggest ambition is to be on the Grand Ole Opry. Hooray! Finally, somebody who doesn't want a country hit so he can cross over!" She knew she had at last found the genuine article, someone who really loved country music.

Martha knew she was "going to get some grief" for signing him because "the general prevailing feeling was that nothing that country would work." She didn't really know how to sign an act to the label, corporate bureaucracies being what they are. Finally, she called the corporate business affairs office and said she was signing a new act. She liked Randy but she did not want to stick her neck out too far; the contract was for four singles. (Most country acts are signed like this—the label commits to singles first and, if these work, then does an album.)

The name *Randy Ray* posed some problems. Nick Hunter, head of promotion for the label, nixed it, saying it sounded "like someone on Podunk Records." Martha came up with *Travis.* "I wanted something he would be comfortable with. I just thought it sounded good and was close to Traywick," she said, adding that "it just came to me."

Randy had not been particularly thrilled about changing his name from Traywick to Ray, and was even less pleased with *Travis.* Finally, he said, "I can live with it."

Lib was enthusiastic about the change—about anything that would finally get Randy on a major label, really. Martha liked Lib from the beginning, sensing she was "shrewd." She got the impression that Lib felt that somewhere along the line she would have to bring someone else in for management, but that was a little further down the line. Right now, the important thing was to get Randy on records.

CHAPTER 16

*R*andy's first recording session for Warner Brothers came on January 30, 1985. He sang four songs: "Prairie Rose," "On the Other Hand," "Carrying Fire," and "Reasons I Cheat." Randy's contract with Warner Brothers was officially signed after this session, on February 14.

"Prairie Rose" went on a soundtrack album for *Rustler's Rhapsody,* a Warner Brothers movie starring Patrick Wayne, John Wayne's son. Ironically, the Duke himself had been in Nashville to record an album in 1973; that recording took place in what is now Nineteenth Avenue Sound, just across the street and about a hundred yards down the block from the Warner Brothers offices.

Steve Dorff, a well-known West Coast producer, produced the rest of the soundtrack album, which featured recordings by other Warner Brothers acts such as Gary Morris, John Anderson, the Nitty Gritty Dirt Band, and Pam Tillis in addition to Randy's cut. Randy's session was produced by Keith Stegall and Kyle Lehning.

74

Lehning, from Cairo, Illinois, was not really a traditional country music fan. He had originally worked as an engineer at the Glaser Brothers Studio when he first came to Nashville in the early 1970s, working with the Glasers, Kenny Rogers and the First Edition, Shel Silverstein, Willie Nelson, and Waylon Jennings. In the mid-1970s he had pop success producing England Dan and John Ford Coley, particularly their *Nights Are Forever without You* LP and "I'd Really Love to See You Tonight" single, which reached number one in 1976.

Lehning, an engineer before he had become a producer, had been producing a few acts and engineering for Ronnie Milsap after England Dan and John Ford Coley disbanded. Keith Stegall had asked him to produce Keith's album for Epic.

During one of their sessions Keith had pulled out a tape and said, "You really ought to hear this." It was the *Randy Ray Live* album, which Keith had produced. Kyle was impressed by Randy's voice and knew that here was a rare talent. Keith told him he ought to go hear Randy at the Nashville Palace. When Kyle did, he was even more impressed to realize that the voice he was hearing live was the same one he heard on tape—no gimmicks, just straight-ahead talent.

Keith suggested Kyle work with Randy to try to get a label deal, but although Kyle liked him, it was a thought he put on the back burner. Then one day, while he was at a publishing company listening to songs for Dan Seals, another act he was producing (and the "England Dan" of the duo he had produced), he got a phone call from Charlie Monk, who told him that Martha Sharp had been to the Palace to hear Randy and that Warner Brothers was interested in signing him. Monk urged Kyle to call Martha to "tell her what you think."

Kyle called Martha immediately to say he liked Randy's talent and would like to produce him if she was interested.

This intrigued Martha because she knew Kyle was not a big country music fan. But she liked Kyle's productions and, after thinking it over, gave him the go-ahead. Keith Stegall would also be involved as a coproducer, something he and Martha had discussed at the Nashville Palace when they went to see Randy perform.

After that first session Keith told Kyle he had to bail out of the production deal. Keith was trying to be a songwriter and an artist and have a family life, too. Besides, it was getting awkward listening to songs from publishers for both Randy and himself—so Keith turned the reins over to Kyle.

Kyle and Randy get along well in the studio. Kyle notes that Randy is easy to produce for several reasons: first, he has incredible talent, and second, he has a firm sense of who he is. From the very beginning Randy knew what kind of songs worked for him and the kind of material he should cut. He was not enamored with the pop world, hoping for pop success while cutting country songs. He loved country and that's what he wanted to cut. All those years of singing in clubs had taught him which songs worked best from the stage and what type of songs he could sing best. That combination makes a producer's job much easier.

"On the Other Hand" had been played for Martha Sharp by song plugger Pat Higdon. Martha liked the song, but had no act for it at the time. Later Kyle and Randy found the song, and all agreed it would be on the first session. It was written by Don Schlitz—who wrote "The Gambler" for Kenny Rogers, "Rockin' with the Rhythm of the Rain" for the Judds, and "Midnight Girl in a Sunset Town" for the Sweethearts of the Rodeo—and Paul Overstreet. According to Schlitz, the two were working on a line in the song "Greedy Heart" when he said to Overstreet, "Well, on the other hand . . ."

Overstreet fired back, "There's a golden band."

Schlitz then countered with, "To remind me of someone who would not understand."

It went back and forth like this for about twenty minutes, and the song was finished.

The two were so sure they had a hit that they were sure a name singer like Merle Haggard or George Jones would record it. They were disappointed to learn Warner Brothers had given it to some newcomer.

That newcomer appeared on "Nashville Now" for the first time as Randy Travis on May 17, 1985. Other guests on that show were banjo whiz Mike Snider, Lorrie Morgan, and Johnny Russell, who introduced Randy by saying, "I believe he's going to be one of the biggest stars in country music." Randy, appearing in a light suit with a dark shirt, sang "Prairie Rose."

When he joined Ralph Emery, Randy said he had seen the movie *Rustler's Rhapsody* a few days before and that it was "a very funny western," although "not quite as crazy as *Blazing Saddles.*"

Ralph brought up the fact that Randy had been on the show before, but under a different name. Randy explained that he had agreed to the change when he signed with Warner Brothers.

"Well, it was their idea," said Randy. "They came up with the idea of wanting to change it, so I went along with it, and I've gotten used to it now."

The first single for Warner, "On the Other Hand," was scheduled to be released in a few months, but Randy didn't do it on the show because, as he admitted, "I don't know it yet." He sang instead a song Johnny Russell wrote that was a hit for Gene Watson, "Got No Reason Now for Going Home." After he finished, Ralph asked why he was singing a song Russell wrote, and Randy replied, "He told me he'd sit on me if I didn't."

Randy's August 6, 1985, appearance on "Nashville Now" was notable for several reasons. First, "On the Other Hand" had just been released, and he performed it for the first time before a national audience. Second, he created quite a stir when he presented Ralph Emery with a plate of food he had cooked for him. The plate, containing shrimp, steak, and lobster that Randy had fixed at the Palace before coming over, was soon taken from Emery by "Nashville Now" piano player Jerry Whitehurst, who ate all the food except for the one shrimp Ralph managed to salvage.

On this show Randy also sang "Always Late," the Lefty Frizzell hit that had been rejuvenated by Dwight Yoakam. His hair was cut shorter and combed back; previously he had worn it longer, over his ears, and parted in the middle.

During the segment of the show where viewers phoned in questions, someone asked Randy a question he was to be asked a number of times—was his father Merle Travis? Randy, of course, was not really a Travis at all and consequently no relation to the great guitar picker and songwriter who composed "Sixteen Tons," "Dark as a Dungeon," and other classics. Still, he had embarked on a career that, like that of his unrelated namesake, would touch millions of listeners with a combination of fresh originality and a faithfulness to the bedrock traditions of country music.

CHAPTER 17

$\mathcal{N}$ ot only do many of the Music Row folks dislike country music, they also dislike country people.

This is most evident at Fan Fair, when twenty thousand country fans come from all over the country to visit Nashville and hear country music. Most of the Music Row executives look down on these "squirrels," as they call them, and avoid them. There's a tremendous irony here. First, these fans buy the recordings that pay these executives' salaries. Second, you would think that when this many fans come to town, it would provide an excellent chance to ask them questions about things the executives need to know. Instead, they run and hide.

A basic problem with Randy and Lib is that they were always more like the country fans than they were Music Row types.

Country people are not refined. They may gawk at famous and semifamous people. They may lack social skills and social graces. Or they may be unable to make polite small talk that has nothing to do with country music. And they may find it difficult (if not impossible) to relate to or converse with people different from them—richer, smarter, more famous—without appearing awkward. For people in the big-time show-biz fast lane, country folks are just plain embarrassing to have around.

But these fans are good people—hardworking, patriotic, meat-and-potatoes-type people. The kind who, if they came over to your house for dinner, would help with the dishes afterward.

Lib and Randy fall into this group. Someone noted about them in their early days in Nashville, "When you stopped talking about Merle Haggard or George Jones, the conversation just drifted away," adding with a touch of sarcasm that "you always knew you weren't talking to nuclear physicists."

Country people live in a limited world, with no desire to transcend those limits. For these people, country music is a way of life, a way of defining who they are and what they are. It's more than just a music to these people: it's a soundtrack for their lives.

The 1985 Fan Fair featured a performance by Randy Travis as part of the Warner Brothers show on Wednesday afternoon, June 12. The fans were sitting in their seats, listening to whoever took the stage and sang. "On the Other Hand" had not been released yet, and very few in the audience had ever heard of Randy Travis or had any idea who he was; but when he performed, there was spontaneous applause in the middle of the song.

In the VIP section, Bob Merlis, head of publicity at Warner's Los Angeles office, came to his feet. At last, he told Martha Sharp, here's a great country singer from Nashville. He wanted to have his picture taken with this guy.

That was the first indication that Randy Travis had a unique appeal to country music fans. When Martha Sharp signed him she had a feeling that "that's what country music is about." She knew that "people get a relationship in their minds with an artist. He's got to be accessible and somebody they care about." She had felt when she first saw him at the Palace that he "looked like a star" and that he was "lovable."

And here was the proof on stage at Fan Fair. These fans were loving Randy Travis because he was singing a great country song with a great voice. But he was also "lovable," and the reaction to him was instantaneous. The fans felt they had found someone worthy of being a star, and they were going to make him one.

Randy and Lib had a booth for the first time this Fan Fair. Randy also spent some time at the Nashville Palace and Warner Brothers booths, signing autographs and meeting fans.

"On the Other Hand" debuted on the charts on August 31 and remained for twelve weeks, rising to number sixty-seven before falling off. Randy and Lib worked hard to make sure it would get some attention, and some early reviews were promising.

Just before the release Randy appeared on the Music Country Radio Network with Charlie Douglas. On July 19 Lib and Warner Brothers hosted a special party for industry folk at the Nashville Palace. Then Randy hit the road, visiting radio stations in Atlanta and getting to know the people at the Atlanta office of Warner Brothers. They were helped here by Ann and Tiny Tant and Ann's mother, Mama Wynette, who gave them encouragement.

There were some promising breaks with songwriting, too. Keith Stegall had recorded "Heaven's Gonna Miss You Tonight," a song he and Randy co-wrote, on his CBS album, and Jeanne Pruett had recorded "I Told You So."

A single on a major label like Warner Brothers was the big break they had been looking for, and both Lib and Randy were determined to capitalize on it. They were pushing and scratching for whatever recognition they could get, determined to launch a career with this single. Both were disappointed when it died at number sixty-seven; Lib was beside herself with frustration and exasperation. She had believed so strongly that country music stardom was just around the corner for Randy; she had given years of her life to this dream, and now she was being proven wrong.

After "On the Other Hand" left the charts, Warner released the next single, "1982." Originally titled "1962," the song came from Atlanta songwriters Buddy Blackmon and Vip Vipperman. Since Travis was only three years old in 1962, and, as he explained, "it would be kind of hard to have a love affair when you're three years old," the title was updated twenty years.

Four people sit together to select songs for Randy Travis: Randy, Lib, Martha Sharp, and Kyle Lehning. When they were listening to "1982" for the first time, Randy made the comment, "Sounds like a Lefty song."

Kyle looked at him blankly and asked, "Lefty who?"

Lib almost fell off her seat while Randy stared back in disbelief. "Lefty. You've never heard of Lefty Frizzell?" Kyle admitted the name sounded familiar, but he couldn't remember hearing anything by him. Randy later made a cassette of Lefty's greatest hits and gave it to Kyle. "Here," he said, handing it to Kyle. "You need to listen to this."

Kyle did.

CHAPTER *18*

andy Travis's star finally began to rise in 1986.

For starters, his second single, "1982," was released in December 1985, so it began the new year on the charts. It rose to number six, staying on the charts for twenty-four weeks before Warner rereleased "On the Other Hand," which returned to the charts on April 26 and landed in the number-one slot on July 26. In between, some major milestones were reached.

At the first of the year Randy still had his job in the kitchen of the Nashville Palace and was singing there as well. But he was also increasingly getting bookings out of town. On some bookings he opened shows for people like T. G. Sheppard and Barbara Mandrell; on others he went out to a club where he played with a house band.

Those are horrible gigs. You show up in a strange town and hope the band knows some of the same songs you do. Often you have little time to rehearse; worse, some house bands have no desire to rehearse. They are celebrities in their own little world, and the visiting artist is an intruder; they have no desire to make him look good.

All those years of playing in clubs worked well for Randy in these situations. He knew a lot of standards, songs that almost every band that plays cover tunes knows—and for most bar bands cover tunes (other people's hits) are their bread and butter.

But even knowing all those songs and having years of experience in clubs didn't help Randy in every situation. One night the only rehearsal he was able to have with the house band consisted of a discussion in the back room. Randy discovered that the band didn't know most of the songs he did; still, the show went on. Things went so badly that every time the band played a few chords right the bass player would yell, "Aw right!" Finally Randy just gave up and started laughing. There was nothing else left to do; humor works better than despair in such a situation.

In an interview with Tommy Goldsmith of the Nashville *Tennessean* in February, Randy said that on these club dates he did three or four songs he had written, but generally, "I don't do anything too complicated. It kinda hurts when they stop playing on you."

Life in an apartment on Music Row was taking its toll. Randy admitted that "I'd like to be able to have horses and a dog again. I'd like to be able to sleep some place where you didn't hear cars going by outside all night long."

Opening for an established artist is a good way for a new artist to get important exposure. The crowds are usually larger, and the distractions of playing in a club—people drinking, dancing, and talking—are usually alleviated. But even this is not all bright lights and glory.

When Randy appeared with Barbara Mandrell in Milwaukee it was his first chance to open for a major act with his own band. In order to do the gig, he and Lib drove twelve hours, managed to get about three hours' sleep in a motel, then went to the concert hall, where he ran through a sound check and rehearsal.

Right after the show they jumped back in the car and drove twelve hours back to Nashville. Randy admitted that "sleeping in the back seat of that car don't get it. Especially when you got luggage back there with you." It earned him some time on the chiropractor's table.

Writer Michael Bane caught up with Randy and Lib in a honky-tonk in Chattanooga early in 1986. Before Randy's performance, the house band alternated with a disc jockey playing disco records. Randy was sick, sipping tea and talking in a whisper. But he could see a light at the end of the tunnel, and during their conversation Randy smiled, shook his head, and said, "It's gonna work. It's really gonna work."

Back in Nashville, Randy was spending time at the Palace with a growing number of music business acquaintances and associates, and on Music Row, writing songs, alone and with others, and singing on demos. He attempted to write with his friend Johnny Russell, but the session didn't turn out as planned. He went to Russell's house for dinner one night, and the two started a song. Russell said to Randy, "Where's your guitar? I'm going to show you how to write a song." But when they went into the den Johnny turned a ballgame on the TV and then fell asleep in the chair.

In March, with "1982" on the charts and a number of offers to play out of town on the books, Randy and Lib finally quit their jobs at the Nashville Palace. It was a big decision, one Randy agonized over. But the calls for club dates were coming in regularly, and he would not be able to do both.

During this same month a big dream came true for him: he performed on the Grand Ole Opry. Introduced by Little Jimmie Dickens, he sang the old Hank Williams gem "I'm So Lonesome I Could Cry" and received a rousing ovation. He admitted to being "scared to death" while standing on that section of the stage where boards from the old Ryman Auditorium had been inserted into the stage of the new Opry House.

He had made it to the stage of the Grand Ole Opry—a goal he had stated back in 1977 after he won the talent contest at Country City USA in Charlotte. Back then he'd said he would know he had made it when he played the Opry. Now he knew there was more to it than that, but at least he had passed this important milestone.

Randy had another significant professional engagement the night after the Opry performance. The Country Radio Seminar attracts influential disc jockeys, programmers, and station owners from all over the United States. The New Faces show, traditionally held after a big banquet on the final night, features performances of all the top new talent who had debuted on the chart that year. There are rules and criteria for eligibility for the show, but Randy didn't meet them—"On the Other Hand" needed to do better, and "1982" was too recent for their consideration deadline. But Charlie Monk, who regularly emcees the event, bent the rules and got Randy a spot. This allowed him to perform and put him right in front of the people who needed to hear him most: the people who decide what's played on country radio. He wowed them.

Randy's Opry performance on March 7 was the realization of a major personal goal, and the New Faces show gave him essential exposure to radio bigwigs. But the biggest event in his professional career so far would take place in April.

CHAPTER 19

*R*andy had been nominated by the Academy of Country Music in the "New Male Vocalist" category. He and Lib flew to Los Angeles to be at the show.

Randy had to arrive at the Goodtime Theater at Knott's Berry Farm several days early to tape his segment of the show. The other nominees—Keith Whitley, Marty Stuart, Billy Burnette, and T. Graham Brown—also taped their segments to be inserted into the live telecast.

At the awards show Randy wore a classic black tuxedo. This was in marked contrast to T. Graham Brown, who wore a purple print suit, Billy Burnette in L.A. Cowboy style, Marty Stuart in total black, and Keith Whitley in a formal gray cutaway.

Randy had met Stuart and Brown before, in Nashville, but this was his first time to meet Whitley or Burnette. Randy and T. Graham had come from Texas to L.A. on the same plane, and Brown had been his usual frisky self, "definitely not boring," according to Randy, so that by the end of the flight "everybody on it knew who we were!"

After the pretelecast taping Randy caught another plane to San Jose, where he opened a show for George Strait, then back to L.A. to open for Strait at the Wiltern Theater. Randy, who was finding a traditional country audience at these appearances, commented that he and Strait "do the same kind of music, so I think we draw the same kind of people."

Randy had met George the previous October, during the ASCAP awards ceremony in Nashville for the top country songs. As he approached Strait to introduce himself, he was shocked and nearly speechless when George turned around, extended his hand, and said, "Hi, Randy. I like your music." Now the two were getting to know each other a little better as they talked on Strait's bus after the shows.

Strait's Los Angeles show was on Saturday night; on Sunday Randy went to Dodger Stadium and watched Los Angeles beat the Giants. On Monday, April 14, was the Academy telecast.

About twenty minutes before showtime, executive producer Dick Clark announced that the show was going to be delayed thirty minutes: President Reagan would be going on television to announce his decision to bomb Libya. Clark's announcement brought a round of sustained applause from the country gathering.

The show finally got underway fifty minutes late. This did not help soothe Randy's nervousness.

Hosted by Reba McEntire, Mac Davis, and John Schneider, the two-hour show was a bit ragged and suffered from the NBC news division's pressure to bring it in on time.

There were performances that night by the Oak Ridge Boys, George Strait, Alabama, the Judds, Judy Rodman, and the hosts, all of whom, along with Randy and the other New Male Vocalist nominees, were seen in previously taped segments.

Alabama won the Entertainer of the Year honors for the fifth consecutive year, George Strait won the Male Vocalist award, and *Does Fort Worth Ever Cross Your Mind* won the Album of the Year honors. Single of the Year went to Ronnie Milsap for "Lost in the Fifties," which edged out "On the Other Hand." Kitty Wells was given the Pioneer Award, and *Sweet Dreams,* the film biography of Patsy Cline, was voted top country music movie.

Randy was surprised when his name was called for Best New Male Vocalist, admitting later that he thought T. Graham Brown would be the winner. Randy felt a bit overwhelmed, obviously nervous, and perplexed about how to act and what to say.

Almost as soon as he walked off the stage, Lib had the award. It was the day before her birthday, and she was "so excited she wouldn't let go" of it, Randy recalls. "Somebody walked up to me and said, 'This must feel pretty good,'" and Lib immediately replied, "It sure does."

Afterward, Randy did some interviews and posed for a lot of pictures. He attended the Warner Brothers party at the Buena Park Hotel, where he was staying, and met Steve Wariner, Dorothy Ritter (Tex's wife and John's mom), and a host of other celebrities. He admitted he was "seeing stars from all the cameras flashing in my eyes" and that he was "pretty surprised, but it was a nice surprise" to win.

Receiving the award got the attention of journalists. The next day Randy was at Le Parc hotel in West Hollywood while Janice Azrak, Warner Brothers' Nashville publicity head, arranged interviews. In one of these, Randy stated a goal: "I want to have a number-one record—a lot of them— and I want to be out there working the road." Questioned further, he admitted that in the long run, "I don't know what I'd wish for. Libby's really a worker, but I don't really know what her dreams for the future are. I don't even know what mine are."

Stardom was coming on like a fast freight train, and Randy was having to make some quick adjustments. Southern California was a new experience. He admitted, "I need to learn how to get around better. It's so different from any place else I've ever been. I'm from a real small town, and this is like a different world for me. I don't know which way anything is." He was having new experiences and learning about the fast lane. "Eating at some of these places has definitely been a first. I'm not really accustomed to sushi bars or Moroccan food."

His natural awe and naïveté at the music-biz world around him was evident in his surprise that the people in L.A. were so gracious. "I didn't expect the people to be so nice to me, for some reason, but they made me feel very welcome, and I appreciate that."

Back in Marshville, Harold Traywick had taped the show on his VCR. He told a local reporter that Randy had been winning awards "since he was eight or nine years old," but that "this is the biggest he's ever won." Harold added, "This will help [his career], but it was already going good."

Randy still did not have an album out on Warner Brothers, though, and was scheduled to play some more honky-tonks with house bands. He had released only two singles—so the question must arise: How did he manage to win?

There is a knack to winning awards that some performers have and some don't. While it is downright uncharitable to imply that a certain performer may not deserve an award, it still must be admitted that while a lot of great artists never seem to get awards, others carry home loads. The awards process is helped by a good publicity plan for the artist, and Warner Brothers, prodded by Lib Hatcher, was doing well there. Also, the Academy of Country Music is based on the West Coast, as is Warner Brothers, which has a strong representation in it. Still, in Randy's case there seemed to be a little more to the matter, a spooky feeling that there was a groundswell of recognition and support for his talent. The promotion staff at Warner Brothers who spend their time on the phone to radio stations were becoming well aware that something big was in the making.

Randy Travis could not be called a star or even an important artist in country music when he won his first major award in April 1986. But things were beginning to change pretty quickly.

CHAPTER 20

*B*efore Randy Travis won his "Hat," as awards from the Academy of Country Music are called, he was just another young country singer trying to get some attention and rise above the crowd. But with this award he began to break out from the pack.

First, he went right back out on the road—he would end up working every day except two in April—and these appearances generated tour publicity.

Most of the day-to-day activity of a publicist in the music industry involves contacting local newspapers in towns where an artist is headed and arranging an interview. Generally the interview is scheduled so the story will run the day of the concert or perhaps a day or two before, generating publicity and enticing people to come out and see the show. This means that most of these interviews are conducted over the phone; the artist calls ahead several days from another town, or while traveling on the road, to talk to a reporter.

Publicists also try to arrange for a reporter to review the concert or perhaps even do a longer, more in-depth story with the artist when they are face to face. The best of these articles and reviews are often put into the artist's press kit to encourage other press media to do stories—successful publicity tends to generate more publicity—as well as add depth and variety to the press kit. This expands it from the basic biography (called a *bio*) and the black-and-white glossy 8 × 10 that are the staples of every artist's press kit.

Randy's performances were gradually progressing from playing club dates wherever he could to regularly opening for major country music acts to becoming a headliner himself. During the spring and summer of 1986 he opened for Conway Twitty, the Statlers, George Strait, George Jones, Ronnie McDowell, and Barbara Mandrell, as well as playing clubs like the Mule's Lip in California, Fool's Gold in Louisiana, and the Buckboard Country Music Showcase in Smyrna, Georgia.

Along the way, Randy and Lib changed the way they traveled. First, Randy hired a five-piece band so he would not have to be dependent on a club's house band or the band of a headline country act. It consisted of Drew Sexton on keyboards, Rick Wayne Money on lead guitar, Rocky Thacker on bass, Gary Carter on steel, David Johnson on fiddle, and Tommy Rivelli on drums, with Sexton, Thacker, and Money providing vocal harmonies. Then they bought a bread truck (which they converted into a band bus by building in five bunks), a van for Randy and Lib, and a horse trailer for their equipment. This new mode was a necessity because, as Randy admitted, "It's no fun trying to travel and sleep in a car. I had to do something. We were on the road so much. I was losing so much sleep."

Even traveling in the van wasn't ideal, though. "It's not real restful, but it sure beats sleeping in the backseat of a car." The van's bed was "not the most comfortable place in the world, but when I'm tired enough I can sure sleep on it."

Things were moving fast for Randy: "I'll tell you, making it in this business has been what I expected for the most part. I enjoy picking and singing, but sometimes you lose a lot of sleep on the road. So much that sometimes you just walk around in a daze. We just played in New York, and then we had to drive to Pennsylvania, and then to Louisville, Kentucky, and back to Nashville, and then to Jacksonville, North Carolina, and then to South Carolina. You lose a lot of sleep just getting from one place to the next. I just hope it keeps on happening. I want to tour throughout the year. This is what I love to do. I do miss home a little, my parents and brothers and sisters, and just being in the country. But I'm happy picking and singing."

His club dates were getting good reviews. In Abilene, Texas, critic Richard Horn wrote, "Between songs, the long, lanky singer relied on his long years of singing in bars to work the crowd by telling mother-in-law jokes and harassing members of his five-piece band. It was all done in that low, slightly burred-edge voice. The young rising star has the same manner of the late, great Jim Reeves and the wardrobe of Ray Price and Eddy Arnold."

In clubs it was noted that Travis "would wear out the dancers with a bunch of heel-scorching numbers and then slow it down a bit to let the racing two-steppers catch their breath. . . . The floor stayed full during both of Travis's sets." At one of his performances it was reported he was wearing "a plum jacket, pinstripe trousers, gold chains, and a diamond ring in the shape of a guitar."

The transition from clubs to concerts was one of the biggest changes Randy had to make. In the concerts, Randy noted, "People aren't drinking and they are listening to every word you sing." He had gotten comfortable singing in clubs, and he was good at it. He would generally open with

Merle Haggard's "Let's Chase Each Other Round the Room" and sing country hits like "Good Hearted Woman," "Waltz across Texas," "He Stopped Loving Her Today," and "I've Been Around Enough to Know" and a Hank Williams medley. He sang his two hits, "1982" and "On the Other Hand," as well as "Can't Stop Now" (the B side of his first single) and a couple of songs from his Nashville Palace album—usually "Send My Body," "Reasons I Cheat," and "Ain't No Use."

Randy was playing four and five nights a week, but was booked only two months in advance. His popularity and demand meant that his rates kept rising. Lib was shrewd enough to realize that if an engagement was confirmed six or eight months in advance, they would have to book it at the current price. And that price might have doubled, tripled, or even quadrupled by the time the date came around.

Randy told Joe Edwards of the Associated Press, "It's a little hard to believe. You work and you work and you work, and then when it happens, it happens so fast. It's overwhelming at times." To another reporter he admitted, "At times it seemed like it would never happen. But then it happened real quick. It's kind of hard to believe."

CHAPTER 21

Warner Brothers rereleased "On the Other Hand" at the end of April 1986. It was a decision opposed by some in the company, but in the end it would prove to be a brilliant move.

The person responsible for picking which singles will be released is Nick Hunter, Warner's head of national country promotion. He receives input from a variety of people, but in the end the decision is his own.

With his Oakland A's baseball cap, jeans, and T-shirt, Nick does not look like one of the most astute men in the country music industry. But looks are deceiving, and Nick has shown a talent time and again for picking hits and bringing them home.

Nick wanted to rerelease the single because he didn't feel Randy had recorded another song strong enough to be a single after "1982." And there were rumblings at the company: the promotion staff was amazed that Randy was finding such incredible acceptance from country music fans. Seemingly independent of promotion's efforts, the fans simply liked Randy Travis and requested his records.

Although "On the Other Hand" had only reached number sixty-seven, there were significant sales orders for the record—a strong indication of consumer demand—and the record had stayed on the charts twelve weeks, an incredible amount of time for a record that climbed no higher than it did.

Kyle Lehning was urging Warner to rerelease the song. He knew about the sales and he also knew it had gone number one in Meridian, Mississippi. He also knew it was a great performance of a great song and, as he stated, "I just didn't think I could make a better record on a better song." Kyle had offered Martha Sharp a deal: if Warner would rerelease "On the Other Hand," they could take the promotion money out of his royalties. Fortunately for Kyle, she did not take him up on his offer.

A strong rumor had it that George Strait wanted to record the song. Everyone at the label agreed that if Strait released it, it would be a smash—a smash that should have belonged to Randy Travis.

Nick made some calls and discovered there were twelve hundred copies of the single stored in Chicago. He ordered them sent to the "A" list, or the *Billboard* reporters, of radio stations. But there weren't enough singles pressed for the entire mailing list of over two thousand stations. Nick wasn't totally convinced this was the best move anyway. After all, one of his field promotion people had called him and warned that this move would "kill Randy's career."

On the first time out, "On the Other Hand" had met with resistance from some country stations, who said it was "too country." But those who played it found something remarkable happening: the fans loved it and lit up the phone lines with requests.

Those on Music Row and in country radio are not known for their modesty and reticence; it is a fact of life that huge egos permeate the whole music business. And decision makers at all levels are convinced they have the power to make or break stars. But there are others who will admit that "Howard and Ethel"—the country music fans—are really the ones who make or break stars. It doesn't matter how much money the record labels spend on an act or how much the radio stations love to play it, if the consumers don't buy the records, it ain't goin' nowhere. Many an artist has been the darling of the music industry, but few have captured the hearts of the country fans. And there have also been cases where the record industry was not enamored with artists that the fans loved—and those artists became stars.

It's not that the music industry didn't like Randy Travis. It's just that the fans realized what an incredible appeal he had and made him a star before the industry caught on. That kind of surprise is pleasant, and country radio and Music Row are smart enough to appreciate a once-in-a-lifetime talent when it comes along.

"On the Other Hand" reached the number-one spot on *Billboard*'s country singles chart on July 26. Meanwhile, Randy's debut album, *Storms of Life*, had been released June 2 and was selling briskly—100,000 copies the first week.

Country music has been characterized as full of "cheatin'" songs, but there are also a lot of anti-cheating songs. "On the Other Hand," which opens the album, is an almost-cheating song—the singer is tempted, but doesn't succumb.

"The Storms of Life," written by Troy Seals and Max Barnes, is a honky-tonk two-step full of picturesque images about a man blown apart by life's storms. In "My Heart Cracked (But It Did Not Break)," a Texas swing number, a jazzy lead guitar counters a story of resilience, a man who rises above heartache.

"Diggin' Up Bones" adds the word "exhuming" to the lexicon of country lyrics as Randy sings about dredging up the past over a ¼ bass-drum sound popularized by Waylon Jennings. "No Place Like Home" conveys the intensity of the singer's love for the home from which his estranged partner has banished him. A verse that is almost a recitation leads into a chorus whose melody ironically recalls "Home Sweet Home."

"1982" is stone country, with a lyric about a man looking at a lost love in his personal rearview mirror. A jukebox jewel, complete with crying steel and a full-strum sock-rhythm guitar, it's the kind of country song that lends itself to being called "classic."

"Send My Body," reprised from the Nashville Palace album, is Randy's up-tempo song about a life of crime paying him off. "Messin' With My Mind" begins with a Merle Travis–style guitar, with finger picking and string bending. There is a clarinet lead and the influence of Merle Haggard—and through him, the country big band sound of Bob Wills—is apparent. The clarinet solo and the melody suggest Jimmie Rodgers. The western swing feel is also reminiscent of Ernest Tubb and his Texas Troubadours during their heyday.

Another of Randy's tunes, "Reasons I Cheat," also comes from the Nashville Palace album. A lonesome fiddle and crying steel introduce this story of an unfaithful man pleading his case; Randy's voice communicates his resignation and regrets.

The final song could be an anthem for country music; it certainly contains Randy and Lib's philosophy and vindicates their belief in traditional country music. "There'll Always Be a Honky Tonk Somewhere" expresses the undeniable belief that while big changes are always happening, human nature stays the same—namely the immutability of human suffering. That means there'll always be a place for traditional country music. It is a jukebox song, with a two-step shuffle until the end, when it modulates and finishes with a walking bass and finally a fadeout.

The message is clear: some things never change. There'll always be a honky-tonk and there'll always be a place for traditional country music, forever and ever. Amen.

The album cover for *Storms of Life* was photographed at an abandoned store in Flynn's Lick in rural Jackson County, Tennessee, between the two small towns of Difficult and Defeated. After the photo session, which lasted past dark, Randy and Lib got lost on the narrow, winding back roads in those mountains and wondered if they'd ever find their way back to Nashville.

On the back of the album Randy thanked "Mama and Daddy, who always believed and cared" and dedicated the album to Lib "for believing when at times it seemed hopeless, for always caring, and for work that should have taken ten people, but was done by one."

Left: Young Randy Traywick, fifteen years old, was already skipping school and getting into trouble with the law. He was increasingly using drink and drugs and wreaking havoc in and around Marshville. This was taken just before he dropped out of school. *Below:* The Traywick brothers (left to right), David, Randy, and Ricky, in the den of their home before some of the trophies and ribbons won in local talent shows and fiddler contests. Their father, Harold, built this 20-by-40-foot room on the back of the house, with a small stage at one end and two jukeboxes, so the boys would have a place to practice and perform. (Photo courtesy of Kate Mangum)

The Traywick home sits on Olive Branch Road, just north of Marshville. Here Harold and Bobbie Rose raised their six children on a farm. (Photo: Don Cusic)

In the spring of 1977, Randy won the talent contest at Country City USA and met his future manager, Lib Hatcher. Here he is shown in a photo taken at home just after he won this contest. (Photo courtesy of Kate Mangum)

The Traywick boys often formed local bands. Here is one group, pictured at the Traywick home, when Randy was about fourteen. (Photo courtesy of Kate Mangum)

After Randy moved to Charlotte, Lib Hatcher became his manager and together they began pursuing a career in country music. Here is one of the earliest publicity photos taken of Randy, who was about eighteen at this time. (Photo courtesy of Kate Mangum)

Above: Lib Hatcher owned and managed Country City USA, where Randy performed for six years—sometimes six nights a week. Next door to the club is a motel which Randy helped refurbish and rebuild. (Photo: Don Cusic) *Below:* When Randy Travis appears at his booth at Fan Fair during June in Nashville, the crowds are packed. Here he signs autographs and chats with fans who have stood in line hours to meet him. (Photo: Don Cusic)

Left: Kate Mangum gave Randy and his brothers guitar lessons, beginning when Randy was eight. The boys would usually go over to her home once a week for their lessons, which generally consisted of Mrs. Mangum showing them chords and leading them through some country songs. (Photo: Don Cusic) *Below:* Lib Hatcher owned and operated Country City USA when she first heard Randy sing during a talent contest sponsored by the club. She knew as soon as she heard his voice that he was a great singer; soon she became his manager and dedicated her life to making him a star.

You don't just look at the camera during award shows—sometimes you look over at some eager fans calling your name. Randy is young and handsome and makes young girls scream and older women want to mother him. His boyish personality and youthful good looks are key ingredients to his success in country music—attracting young fans to traditional music. (Photos: Don Cusic)

Right: When you're a superstar, you get to hang out with other superstars. Here Randy is shown backstage at the American Music Awards with Janie Fricke and Stephen Stills (Photo: Jammie Arroyo/Retna Ltd.) *Below:* Randy is shown backstage at the Academy of Country Music Awards with Charley Pride and Juice Newton. (Photo: Jammie Arroyo/Retna Ltd.)

Right: Randy loves performing and spends more than two hundred days a year on the road, singing to audiences.

Above: When Randy was singing at the Nashville Palace, Ricky Van Shelton would sometimes come by and sit in with the band. The two singers became friends, with Randy letting Ricky spend some time on stage in front of the Palace audiences, giving Ricky a big break when he was an unknown. (Photo: Beth Gwinn/Retna Ltd.) *Below:* Randy and k.d. lang chat backstage. (Photo: Beth Gwinn/Retna Ltd.)

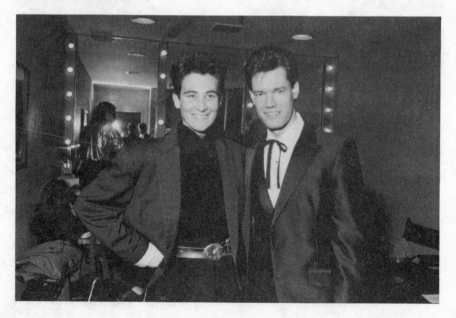

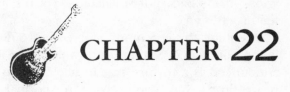

CHAPTER 22

*R*icky Skaggs had been scheduled to read the nominations for the Country Music Association's 1986 awards at the Opryland Hotel. But shortly before, there was a tragedy in Skaggs's life: a truck driver had shot into the car where his six-year-old son was riding, hitting the boy in the neck. Ricky rushed to the hospital and stayed by his side.

With Ricky unable to read the nominations to the assembled press, the CMA contacted Randy, who agreed to come over. Randy said, "It was strange. They don't let you know whose names are going to be called before you get to open the envelope. So there I was reading the nominations, and there was my name coming up four times. It was quite a shock, believe me."

The rereleased "On the Other Hand" had hit number one on the charts, and Randy's fourth single, "Diggin' Up Bones," was climbing quickly (it would reach number one on November 8). *Storms of Life* was selling extraordinarily well.

Randy would not find it difficult to get a ticket to this year's awards show.

It is an awkward position to be in, nominated for a major award. First, the honor of being nominated overwhelms you; then comes the thought of winning. At the same time you must be careful—you can't help calculating your chances of winning while at the same time preparing yourself to lose. You don't want to show disappointment when someone else wins—that's bad sportsmanship—yet it's impossible not to feel a letdown.

Attending the ceremony is even more nerve-racking than being nominated. Sitting there waiting for the winner to be announced is a torture test in itself. If you don't win, your heart drops, but you're back to normal breathing fairly quickly. If you do win, however, the nervousness intensifies because now you have to go on national television and accept the award, saying something intelligent and intelligible in the process.

You don't prepare an acceptance speech because that is too presumptuous—and even feels like bad luck—so you're left gaping unprepared at millions of viewers when you win. You have a lump in your throat, you feel like you're in a daze, and you try to remember everybody or at least the most significant persons; still, after you leave the stage—and especially as you're driving home—you think of things you didn't say but should have, and you start kicking yourself.

The feelings you have—pride, relief, nervousness—are indescribable; you simply can't articulate them. You are immensely proud of winning, relieved you don't have to wonder about it anymore, and incredibly humbled to join the ranks of some of your heroes, knowing all the while that the other nominees deserve this award just as much.

Actually, what you're feeling is a surreal numbness, like this isn't really happening to you. And at the same time it's too good to be true.

It's one thing to have dreams. It's another to have them start coming true.

The Twentieth Annual Country Music Association Awards Show was held Monday, October 13, 1986. Hosted by Willie Nelson and Kris Kristofferson, the show featured performances by Lionel Ritchie and a number of duets: Marie Osmond and Paul Davis, Eddie Rabbitt and Juice Newton, Nicolette Larson and Steve Wariner, and the first interracial duet ever to appear on the country charts, Earl Thomas Conley and Anita Pointer.

Randy took home the Horizon Award that evening. Preceding the award were short clips introducing the artists to the audience. In Randy's clip he was shown working out in a gym, his great love in addition to country music at the time.

Two days after the CMA Awards, on October 15, Randy appeared on "Hee Haw" with Judy Rodman, Danny White, and cohost Mel Tillis. Marshville, with an announced population of 2,177, was saluted from the Hee Haw cornfield.

A lot of dreams were coming true for Randy. One of his biggest came at the end of October. That's when he bought a sixty-three-acre farm near Ashland City, in Cheatham County, about twenty-five miles from Music Row. This little town looks amazingly like Marshville, though the hills are bigger, and has a population about the same. People have been known to drive long distances to eat there because of its reputation of cooking the best catfish in the country, caught in the nearby Harpeth River.

Randy and Lib paid a quarter million dollars for the place, with an old log cabin located at the end of a narrow dirt road. The young singer who eight months earlier was wondering if it was financially wise to quit his cooking job at the Nashville Palace wrote a check for seventy-five thousand dollars to cover the down payment. It didn't bounce.

CHAPTER 23

Perhaps the biggest concert Randy Travis played in 1986 occurred on November 15 in Charlotte, North Carolina. Opening for George Jones (with Patty Loveless also on the bill), Randy was playing in this area for the first time since his days at Country City USA.

Ten thousand fans packed into the Hampton Coliseum, and, as one Marshvillian who attended noted, "Most came to see Randy. George Jones could've stayed home."

In Charlotte Randy received a proclamation from Mayor Harvey Gantt that read, "Whereas in his brief professional career, Randy Travis has already scored two number-one hits, and . . . because of the national recognition he has brought to this area . . . Saturday, November 15, 1986, is hereby proclaimed as Randy Travis Day in Charlotte." It was also proclaimed Randy Travis Day in Marshville through an ordinance adopted by the Marshville town board on November 3.

The reviewer for the show noted that Randy's "inexperience on stage was apparent," but "although his stage presence left something to be desired, Travis's selection of songs didn't disappoint anyone." He added, "All Travis has to do to make anyone realize he's all country is sing."

When Randy sang "On the Other Hand," the reviewer noted, "Every female in the house screamed during most of the song, and Travis's boyish appearance and ever-present grin brought only more approval." He sang his own hits, a Hank Williams medley, and "American Trilogy," a medley of "Dixie," "Battle Hymn of the Republic," and "All My Trials" made famous by Elvis.

Other big changes were taking place in Randy's life. A major performer is not just an individual, he's a whole business. Randy and Lib formed Travis/Hatcher Corporation on November 14, reflecting their new status as money-makers. They also created the Lib Hatcher Agency to help them keep control of their bookings by putting it all in-house.

Previously Randy's engagements had been handled by a Nashville talent agency. Pulling him out of this agency was a potentially risky move. If somehow his star stopped rising and the demand slowed, then other agencies would be reluctant to put him on their roster. It was a move that could easily have backfired on Lib and Randy, but it didn't. Some may have thought at the time that it was bad business, and it certainly ruffled a few feathers, but in the end it proved to be shrewd.

In November Warner Brothers held a party at the Station Inn bluegrass bar on a Tuesday afternoon to honor Randy's *Storms of Life* album, presenting him with a Gold Record. At this party, Randy made a major announcement.

"They've asked me to join the Opry," he said, obviously proud as well as humbled at seeing this lifelong dream come true. "And I think that means more to me than anything else." He added that "Hal Durham (the general manager of the Opry) told me they needed me on the show. Isn't that something?" There was genuine disbelief in his voice.

Randy had taped "Austin City Limits" and was finishing the year with personal appearances that had been booked before the CMA's Horizon Award. At one show, held at the club One Arroyo Place in Harlingen, Texas, on Thanksgiving night, a rare event occurred: the hall was half empty.

He did not get a stellar review of his performance from critic Bruce Lee Smith, either. Travis began his set with "Louisiana Saturday Night," which caused a "mass migration to the dance floor," but after this the show seemed to bog down. Randy was still trying to make the transition from being a club performer to a concert performer.

According to Smith, the major flaw in the show was that Travis "talks too much. Every song seemed to elicit some anecdote from Travis, usually its chart history. As a result, the people on the dance floor got tired of waiting and headed back to their seats."

Another engagement, in October, hadn't turned out too well, either. When word spread that Randy had been booked at the club Ghost Town in the Sky in Waynesville, North Carolina, people traveled from Virginia, Kentucky, Atlanta, Tennessee, Greenville, and Spartanburg to see him. About thirty-five hundred persons showed up. One man purportedly drove six hours and another drove six hundred miles, but when they got there, the doors were locked and Randy Travis wasn't even in town. It seems the club had been sold and the new owner had ordered it closed for the rest of the season. The fans hadn't heard the news and were pretty upset.

Randy had released a Christmas song, "White Christmas Makes Me Blue." When he came home to visit Marshville in early December, that single had sold over seventy-nine thousand copies. Besides visiting family and friends during this brief visit, Randy spent time riding horses with his dad and other family members and ate breakfast one morning at Little Tom's Cafe on East Union Street. He had just appeared on Joan Rivers's talk show and the "Today" show and admitted that "I've averaged about five days a week (this year) singing. Singing that much and working that much, it wears you out." He admitted to a local reporter that he missed his family and looked forward "to every time I can get down here."

His induction into the Grand Ole Opry occurred Saturday night, December 20, on Ricky Skaggs's portion of the show, which was broadcast live over the Nashville Network. Also appearing on this 7:00 P.M. segment—just before Roy Acuff's slot—were Lorrie Morgan, Jim and Jesse, and the Whites.

On stage, Randy sang "Diggin' Up Bones," obviously feeling nervous, and told the Opry audience, "This is probably one of the biggest, happiest nights of my life, to tell you the truth. It's been an honor just to be able to come backstage and be around some of the great people here at the Grand Ole Opry—people that I've admired for a lot of years, admired their music and loved their music. It's great to be a part of the Opry family now."

Skaggs came out and, looking at Randy, referred to the George Jones hit "Who's Gonna Fill Their Shoes," saying, "Well, I tell you one thing, George. This fella right here, they're gonna be trying to fill his shoes one of these days.

"There's one thing about the kind of music you do," said Skaggs to Travis. "Ain't nobody mistaking it. It sure is country."

CHAPTER 24

R andy finished 1986 with a New Year's Eve concert at the Bay Front Exhibit Hall in Corpus Christi, Texas, with Kathy Mattea. It had been the biggest year of his professional career. *Rolling Stone* had written that "of all the cool new country stars, expect Randy Travis to last the longest."

During an appearance on "Nashville Now" December 12 Ralph Emery had played a clip from the January 1984 show of a very nervous Randy with a shaking microphone. After Randy sang "Diggin' Up Bones" it was announced that *Storms of Life* had sold over 850,000 copies and that he was working on his next album. He also sang his next single, "No Place Like Home," which had just debuted. The year 1986 closed like it had begun, with a hot record climbing up the charts.

"No Place Like Home," written by Paul Overstreet, was scheduled to be Randy's first single accompanied by a video.

Though he had shot the video in September while he was out in California, it hadn't been released.

Randy was beginning to meet his heroes on an equal footing. He had met George Jones after opening the show for him during the summer. Randy said he "got to sit on the bus and talk to him a little bit." He added, "He was very nice to us. It's nice to meet people like that, especially people you've really admired for so long."

Jones had paid Randy a compliment, saying he liked what the young singer was doing. Randy was sitting on the side of the stage watching Jones's portion of the show when George introduced him and brought him back onstage to sing with his band. George played rhythm guitar while Randy was singing, and Travis admits that it "was quite a feeling."

Making the transition from being unknown to somewhat known to finally famous, he confessed in August that "the 'superstar' label still seems kind of new to me, to tell you the truth. I don't know if I ever will get used to it. But it's a nice feeling; it really makes me feel great. I've worked over ten years to have something finally happen, and I'm very proud of what I've done."

Randy had said back in 1977 when he won the Country City USA talent contest, "If I ever get to the stage of the Grand Ole Opry, I guess I'll know that I made it." He had made it to that stage in March 1986 and permanently joined the Opry in December—so there were no doubts there. But there were other milestones that caused him to feel good about his career and his life.

The first was being signed by Warner Brothers the year before. Then, when "1982" began climbing the charts, "I felt like everything was starting to go on the upswing." After he won the Academy of Country Music's award he said, "I don't know how many years I've watched about every awards show that's come on. For years I've thought how nice it would be to win something. When it happened, it was like a dream come true."

On his newfound fame he said, "I try not to take the things that are written about me too seriously, anyway. We just want to get out there and get our music going."

In May, when he played at Gilley's in Pasadena, Texas, Bob Claypool of the Houston *Post* interviewed him in Room 110 of Grumpy's Motor Inn and noted, "So far, he has none of the emotional defenses and ego-shields of a budding 'star.'"

Claypool added that "one longtime Gilley's employee thinks he's going to be the biggest thing since George Strait because he has sex appeal for the women and the hard-core male country fans like him, too."

Travis admitted he was "surprised" by his success, especially the sales of his first album. When sales had reached the 200,000 mark he felt, for the first time, like a significant member of the country music community. But as it continued to sell and even entered the pop charts, his amazement grew.

The success on the pop charts was more than amazing: it was almost confusing. Randy had made it clear since day one that he was not interested in pop success, pledging his allegiance to country music, and here he was singing that stone-country music *and* making it on the pop charts. He remarked that "the pop charts sure is a strange place" for his music. "I couldn't believe it, but I guess when they sell good they automatically go into that chart. Quite a compliment, I guess."

At a press conference after the CMA awards show he was asked, "What is there about Randy Travis that people just love so much?" Randy was befuddled by the question and answered, "I don't have any idea. I never really think about it like that." But he was going to have to start thinking about things like that because the press was trying to figure him out.

He had begun the year working at the Nashville Palace, cooking and cleaning up in addition to his singing chores, and ended it a full-time country artist, traveling with a full entourage. In December Lib replaced their bread truck—and—van arrangement with a Silver Eagle bus she bought from Mickey Gilley. (Later, they would buy another one from Keith Stegall.)

The merchandising offered for sales at concerts had grown from some caps and bandannas carried by Lib in an old blue suitcase to include tapes, T-shirts, bumper stickers, sweatshirts, headbands, key chains, fans, and black-and-white photos.

There had been profiles in the country music publications, *USA Today, Rolling Stone, Newsweek,* the *Wall Street Journal,* and *People;* guest appearances on "Today" and "The Late Show" with Joan Rivers; appearances on the Nashville Network; and stories in newspapers almost everywhere he performed. It was enough to make him a household name.

It had been a busy year; Randy had only about twelve days off in all of 1986. The increased traveling was beginning to make his life a blur. Randy noted, "You go to bed and wake up in a different town. It's hard to keep up with where you're at."

His shows still consisted of a number of other people's songs, like Merle Haggard's "Let's Chase Each Other Round the Room," Waylon and Willie's "Good Hearted Woman" Mel McDaniel's "Louisiana Saturday Night," and Hank Williams's "I Saw the Light." But he was increasingly beginning each concert with a song from his debut album, "My Heart Cracked (But It Did Not Break)," and his own hits began to occupy a larger portion of the concert.

William Kerns of the Lubbock *Evening Journal,* reviewing a concert at the Panhandle South Plains Fair, had proven prophetic when he wrote earlier in the year, "Travis deserves watching. He's really just in the beginning stages of his career, but already he's managing to win over audiences with his easygoing charm, gentle handling of a lyric, and carefully plotted concerts. Heck, there aren't that many musicians who can even tell a joke, and Travis took the time to click on at least two out of three." Altogether, "he offered a terrific concert and managed to show indications he'll be even better after dealing with the scars and seasoning which walk hand in hand with experience on the road."

 # CHAPTER 25

*T*he doors of country music stardom were flung open for Randy Travis in 1986. In 1987 he walked in and took over the room.

In January Randy performed "On the Other Hand" at the Nashville Songwriters Association Awards, televised from the Tennessee Performing Arts Center in Nashville. A week later he appeared on the American Music Awards as he and copresenter Lisa Lisa of Cult Jam handed out the Favorite Country Video award.

In February *Storms of Life* was certified platinum, indicating sales of one million copies. Randy was then getting about sixty cents for each album sold. Warner Brothers grossed approximately $5.2 million from this album. Since it had cost only about sixty-five thousand dollars to produce, the profits were huge.

The Grammy Awards were held on February 24. Although Randy was nominated for Male Vocalist, he didn't win; that honor went to Ronnie Milsap for "Lost in the Fifties Tonight." Randy did perform on the show, however, as sixty-five million people watched. And appearing on a Grammy show is always important, because a good performance could mean album sales of a hundred thousand copies when those viewers visit record stores.

At the Academy of Country Music Awards on April 6, Randy had nearly a clean sweep, winning Male Vocalist, Album of the Year, Single of the Year, and Song of the Year in addition to performing his new single, "Forever and Ever, Amen" on the nationally televised show.

With Reba McEntire winning Female Vocalist, it was obvious that traditional country music was on the upswing. It was also the end of an era: Alabama, who had won more Academy awards than any other act, did not win any this night, losing Group of the Year honors to the Forrester Sisters, thus ending their five-year reign in that category.

In June, at the *Music City News* Awards, Randy won Male Vocalist, Single of the Year, Album of the Year, and the Star of Tomorrow award. This meant that before the year was half over Randy had won eight major awards and had been seen on television by over one hundred million people.

The single "Forever and Ever, Amen" debuted on the *Billboard* charts on April 25; it would reach the number-one position on June 13 and remain there three weeks. This would become what every singer searches for—his "career record," the one that would define him and put him in the upper echelons of stardom. More than any other single recording, this is the song that made Randy Travis a significant country music star in 1987 and for years to come.

Randy's second album, *Always and Forever,* was released on his birthday, May 4, and quickly climbed to number one.

The album begins with "Too Gone Too Long," a Tin Pan Alley–style song about replacing an old love. Punctuated by Mark O'Connor's fiddling and Jerry Douglas's dobro picking, the cut combines the feel of western swing with the instrumentation of bluegrass. "My House," written by Paul Overstreet and Al Gore, the team that wrote "Diggin' Up Bones," is a ballad of true love. Randy's song "Good Intentions," co-written with Marvin Coe, is reprised from the Nashville Palace album.

The up-tempo "What'll You Do About Me" presents the humorous side of a man desperately in love. "I Won't Need You Anymore," by Troy Seals and Max Barnes, begins like "On the Other Hand" with an acoustic rhythm guitar introduction, and, like that first hit, it extols fidelity.

"Forever and Ever, Amen," by Don Schlitz and Paul Overstreet, captures the joy, infused in both the lyrics and melody, of loving someone all of your life. The dancing dobro licks and brushes on the drums give the tracks a back-to-basics feel, while the lyrics articulate the 1980s' new tradition of faithfulness.

"I Told You So," written by Randy, finally makes it appearance on a major label. Arguably his best-written song, it's about a lover's revenge on a partner who thought the grass would be greener on the other side. "Anything" continues the true-love theme of "Forever and Ever, Amen."

The clever wordplay of "The Truth is Lyin' Next to You" precedes "Tonight We're Gonna Tear Down the Walls," co-written by Randy with Jim Sales. You can hear the influence of Hank Williams's "Settin' the Woods on Fire" and Merle Haggard's "Let's Chase Each Other Round the Room"; the western swing of Bob Wills echoes through the instrumental break, with its clarinet lead.

The cover, capitalizing on Randy's sex appeal, is a close-up of him staring seductively at the camera. His newfound affluence is also apparent in his rings and bracelet of gold and diamonds. The cover depicts a sophisticated, sexy male, while the music inside is full of tradition and roots. It is this combination of the contemporary and the timeless that has become the essence of Randy Travis's image and appeal.

Randy had begun recording the second album at the end of 1986. Attempting to repeat the tremendous success of *Storms of Life* must have weighed heavily on Randy and producer Kyle Lehning, but, as Kyle said, "We decided that since we didn't know what we were doing on the first album, we'd just go do it again for the second."

Martha Sharp, Lib, Randy, and Kyle again listened to hundreds of songs. They recorded about twenty and picked what they felt were the best ten. Randy had said, "I try to find ten of the best songs I can possibly find. I don't care who writes them. Just something that is very well written and tells a complete story." He felt that "songs today don't seem to finish the idea. I don't look for specific subject matter. Just something people can relate to."

Like the first album, the actual recording did not take that long—each three-hour session yielded three or four basic tracks. But, as Randy admitted, the time-consuming process was finding the songs, trying them out, deciding which would be best for him.

When *Always and Forever* was finished and before it had come out, Randy was philosophical, saying "I'm done with my part of it. It has crossed my mind that people will be comparing it a lot to the first album." Still, he felt it was a good record, and even if it turned out not to have the sales success of *Storms of Life*, it was work he could be proud of, satisfied he had done his best and comfortable with the music inside.

Randy was still on the road, but the gigs were changing. A year before he was playing clubs that seated about four hundred people and charged six dollars a head. Randy was getting five hundred to a thousand dollars a night for these bookings when he was by himself, and moved up to two to three thousand dollars after he won his first award and got a band. In the first half of 1987, in contrast, Randy was playing halls seating ten thousand persons, each paying fifteen to twenty dollars. His fee rose to about ten to fifteen thousand dollars a night and would continue to climb. He and Lib would also begin promoting some concerts themselves, assuring them of up to 90 percent of the gate for some shows.

The constant touring and singing was taking its toll on Randy's voice. In early 1987 he received laser treatments on his vocal cords from Dr. Robert Ossoff of the Vanderbilt University Medical Center in Nashville. Dr.Ossoff showed him a videotape of his voice charted on a graph and explained the mechanics of singing, teaching him warm-up and breathing exercises that would lessen the strain on his voice. It was important to avoid the dry throat he was suffering from; it was also imperative to protect his voice to avoid the singer's nightmare: losing it altogether.

Randy had never really worked on vocal techniques, intuiting that the key to country music was emotion, not technique. He had told one reporter, "Technically, I know that I'm not one of the greatest singers by far, if you're looking at it from a vocal-coach point of view. But I sure try to sing with a lot of feeling and a lot of emotion, try to make it sound believable. I guess that's what I learned from country singers, from listening all my life to people like Merle Haggard and George Jones, people like Hank, Sr. They sang with such feeling. To me that's what they were all about. They made everything they sing believable, whatever it might have been about, whatever subject."

Right after the Academy of Country Music award ceremony Randy and Lib flew out to New Mexico, where Randy did a small part in a movie. *Young Guns* starred Emilio Estevez, Keifer Sutherland, Charlie Sheen, and Lou Diamond Phillips. After the shooting, which lasted two days, Randy said, "My part was so small they didn't even give me a name." He added, "They have Billy [the Kid] and a lot of guys trapped in this house, and they're having this big shootout. I'm with one of the gang that's standing outside, watching and shooting at them, I guess. This guy comes out and I say 'There's . . .' I can't think of his name now . . . anyway, I say, 'Git 'im,' and this guy standing beside me acts like he don't really want to do it. And then I say, 'Shoot 'im,' and push him to shoot him. That's about all I do. I just give the order."

Randy said "I got to shoot pool and talk with [the other actors] some. They acted like they were really happy to see me there, and they actually seemed to know something about country music. I was real nervous when I did my little part. They gathered round and watched." He found that acting "kinda scared me. I'd rather do something small in something that was very successful than be the whole deal and be a flop."

At the time Randy said, "I'll probably be on the screen for thirty seconds." He feared he would "actually end up looking like a bad guy 'cause I give orders to shoot one of 'em."

But when the movie appeared, Randy didn't even get the small time he thought he would. "I got cut out," he said. "I just stand there and watch them ride away. I was left on the editing floor." Though there isn't much of Randy to see in the movie, there's more to hear: he, Lib, and John Lindley wrote the title song.

Back in North Carolina, Harold and Bobbie Rose went to see the movie and left thinking Randy wasn't in it at all. With Randy made up to look like a dusty saddle tramp with long sideburns and drooping mustache, and his part only a few moments of looking at some departing cowboys, not even his own parents recognized him on the big screen.

CHAPTER 26

While he was on the road, interviewers often asked Randy about country music and its future. Never a really deep thinker or one with any pretensions to intellectualism, he was not used to thinking about such things. Simply put, he was a singer and an entertainer—he knew songs to sing and how to work a crowd in a club. That's what he studied, that's what he practiced; philosophies and theories didn't really enter into it. Yet increasingly he was called upon to be a spokesman for country music and to articulate the trend of new traditionalism.

New traditionalism is an oxymoron if there ever was one. The term represents an attempt by the country music industry to cover its tracks and create the illusion that "tradition" could somehow be "new."

Randy presented a slightly different picture, a version born out of politeness but also frustration that the music he loved—and the people he and Lib are—had been scorned by the country music industry for years.

Randy told one reporter, "I'm just part of the traditional country that is making a good comeback. I don't know why it's been a success for me. I love what I'm doing. That's the type of music I love to do, and it's all I can do.

To another reporter he confessed, "To tell you the truth, I don't feel like I could do anything else. Your voice has to fit the stuff you do, and I think I would sound funny doing anything else." He told a number of others, "I've never wanted to sing anything else," adding, "That's all I've ever really known. I grew up listening to people like George Jones and Merle Haggard. And when I started playing, I wanted to play that way. There's a feeling in the best country songs and the best singers that can't be faked. That's what I've always worked for—to capture that feeling."

When questioned about singing pop, he said, "I guess you definitely won't hear me on any pop records. I just couldn't do it. I can't—not this voice. I never listened to that kind of music. You won't hear me with any crossover hits. I'm pure country."

On the early turndowns in Nashville he said, "To tell the truth, I did get turned down by every label in town at first. They never did say why. But I think it's better that I did have a long time before the album. Those fourteen years I spent in clubs have prepared me vocally and personally for the success now."

About traditional country music's audience Randy said, "I think there's always going to be that group of people that like it, and not necessarily a small group of people."

As for being labeled a new traditionalist, he replied, "It suits me fine. That's what I am, and that's the kind of music I'm doing." But about being considered "too country" by some stations he said, "Some radio stations still won't play my music because they say I'm 'too country.' But if they call themselves country stations, there's no reason they shouldn't." He told another, "If you're supposed to be a country radio station, it seems kind of dumb for anyone to be 'too country.'"

Randy observed, "Music is always changing. But I believe [the traditional style of] country music will always be there—at least I sure hope so. It's just a real music. It really deals with things that people go through in everyday life."

He stated his view that "I think there have always been people out there who wanted to hear that kind of music, but it seems like all the artists got to wanting to cut crossover music. I think the artists just got so wrapped up in crossover music they forgot about the real country, and if it hadn't been for Merle Haggard and George Jones, you wouldn't of heard it for awhile. I started at an early age, and that's all I've ever listened to, all I've ever sung. It's just what I do. It's all I care to do."

Then Randy added, "Don't get me wrong. I like all the music I hear on the country radio stations, even the stuff that ain't country. But I think there's a lot of artists that have gotten all wrapped up in cutting crossover songs that . . . well, I don't want to say anything bad. I'd just hate to see it get to the point where I can't turn on the radio and listen to someone like Merle Haggard."

Bill Ivey, executive director of the Country Music Foundation, observed that "country music has its greatest impact on pop culture when someone comes along who is true to the music's historical integrity in a way that would make you think he'd appeal only to hard-core fans, but also has the personal magnetism to reach out and hit noncountry fans emotionally. Travis is certainly not the first person in recent years to revitalize traditional country, but I think he is the first one with that kind of potential pop charisma."

Jack Hurst, in his column in the *Chicago Tribune*, summed it up best at the end of 1986. He stated, "Great traditional country music, especially when performed by a youngster, can have more marketplace impact than the bland, generic, 'contemporary' country sound everybody bowed down to for a decade hoping for 'crossover' sales."

CHAPTER 27

*P*eople who go from obscurity to stardom in a short time are fond of saying that they haven't changed at all. That's partly true, but it's not necessarily the advantage they proclaim it to be.

Reporters began asking Randy about changes in himself beginning in 1986, when success started hitting. He told one he didn't think he'd ever get "a swelled head," adding, "I don't think it will happen. I don't plan to change any."

To another who asked if success had changed him he replied, "Well, we have a lot of success, but there again, you know I'd like to think that it hasn't changed me in any way. I would say I'm the same person I've always been and I will always be that same person. I would like to think so, anyway."

And to yet another who asked him about changing he said, "I guess it's easy to see how you could. I just don't see why anybody would." He added, "I guess it's normal for people to think I've changed, but I haven't."

When you become a star, the first people who change are the people around you. They look at you and treat you differently. Even though you are essentially the same—wanting old relationships to continue as before—the situation around you has changed so much that it's virtually impossible.

Strangers come knocking and must be dealt with, newcomers vie to be admitted to the inner circle, and old friends become envious, jealous, and resentful. There is no longer an equality—the star is elevated by money, success, and recognition. And so the relationships start to change.

The next stage is when the performer begins to change. You cannot be the same person who used to play the local bar when you are performing before crowds of ten thousand, being interviewed by the media, appearing on national television, and hobnobbing with other celebrities. The things you talk about and the way you act are now different from the way you used to act and things you used to talk about. And so a performer must grow and rise to a new level. Those who can't, find themselves back at the local bar.

Then there is the fact that the more successful you become, the more others defer to you. Sometimes this is because of status, sometimes because of money. At first you feel uncomfortable in this situation, then you begin to like people anticipating your every need and fetching whatever you wish. Finally, you begin to expect such treatment, feeling it is owed to you because of your star status.

The relationship with fans is equally complex. At first an artist courts fans like a young man courts a young lady, doing anything to please. But, in the end, the star erects barriers against fans—you try to keep them away and limit your exposure to them. Part of this comes from pressures and demand: an artist must have some privacy, but fans want all your time. And it also comes from trying to control your life, convinced somehow you can.

*   *   *

There were some big changes in Randy's professional life in 1987. First, he had gone from being an opening act for country artists to being a headliner. "It's the biggest change I have had to deal with," he said. "I had never traveled much." No longer was he playing in clubs, sitting and talking with people between sets; increasingly, he was being recognized in public and asked for autographs even when he went to eat or shop. People in the spotlight give up their personal lives; no longer are you just a private person when you go out your door—wherever you are you're public property. And the public always wants to check on its property.

The success was startling, and Randy said, "At times it seems like it's somebody else and not me." He took comfort in the fact that people he had known and worked with over the years were still his friends and bandmates. He was especially glad to have Lib still there.

He told one reporter, "I'll tell you what is funny, though. I worked clubs for all those years, from the time I was fourteen, right on up to last year. And we still work a club date now and then. Doing clubs, you're always singing everybody else's hits; Merle Haggard's hits, George Jones's hits, Lefty Frizzell's hits, Hank Williams's hits . . . Then all at once, you get to where you're doing Randy Travis's hits." He grinned in disbelief. "That's weird. Yeah, that's a big change, for sure."

Some personal relationships soured along the way—particularly ones with John Hobbs, Charlie Monk, and Ann Tant. John Hobbs had never been particularly close to Lib and Randy—he was a demanding boss they had to put up with. Randy remembered the humiliations and Lib remembered the long, tough hours. When Randy hit, the Nashville Palace plastered his name and face all over the place. Randy and Lib openly thanked Hobbs; they knew that the exposure there was vital and that the time spent there was important to their development. They made sure the Palace got a Gold Album when *Storms of Life* was certified.

The problems with Charlie Monk centered on his performance as a publisher: Lib charged there had been deception and that he had not adequately fulfilled his role. Monk insisted he had been more than fair and had given them breaks in the early years when they needed it.

There was plenty of bitterness and threats of lawsuits. Lib had looked to Monk for advice and help with management decisions, but Monk wasn't interested in helping the way Lib wanted him to help. Then, when Randy started hitting, Charlie decided he wanted to get on board—and wanted all the action. Lib turned him down in no uncertain terms. When they finally reached a settlement, Randy reportedly gave Monk $200,000 in exchange for the rights to all the songs Randy had written, originally copublished by Monk and their publishing company, Three Story Music.

The misunderstandings between Lib and Ann were as much personal as professional. When Lib hit the big time, Ann thought she should be brought along because Lib "owed" her. But it didn't work that way.

Actually, Lib and Randy did hire Ann to drive the van and sell merchandise in 1986, when the singles were just starting to hit. But Warner Brothers supposedly did not want Ann around since she used to work for them. This came to a head at the Warner Brothers party during the Academy of Country Music awards in 1986. When Lib told Ann she couldn't come to the party, Ann was livid—and that was the end of that friendship. Bitter, Ann set about writing a book exposing Lib's purported double-dealing.

This disagreement between Ann and Lib was the culmination of years of fuming. It is difficult, if not impossible, for two such strong-willed, independent women to live in harmony for long. There was also more than a touch of jealousy because one was now rich and famous while the other was not.

The core of the problem is that their relationship had changed. For years, Ann had been Lib's and Randy's entrée into the country music world, introducing them to stars and key executives, getting them backstage at the Opry. Lib, a little in awe of her, deferred to Ann in the early days. But then Lib became the one with the power. Ann couldn't accept this role reversal, and clashes erupted. Finally, Ann was eased from the scene.

Things like this are not unusual. When newcomers arrive in Nashville knowing nothing about the music industry, they meet people, if they're lucky, who help educate them. Those first contacts can shape the way they perceive Music Row. Along the way, they gain more business connections and learn about other facets of the industry; eventually they come to see that there's more to it than those initial contacts could teach them.

So they must move on. Lib's ambition was such that she didn't stop to smooth all the feathers she ruffled when she moved on to a higher plateau. She was brusque and dismissive, more concerned with finding new avenues of exposure for Randy than with finding ways to repay old favors.

Coming into the industry, you don't start out meeting the people at the top rung of the ladder: they're too busy dealing with others at the top. So you try to find people who are established somewhere in the middle. As you begin to climb, you keep reaching for contact with those still higher up.

There's more to being successful than talent or musical skill: there are character traits as well. It involves an ability to understand people, grace under pressure, and a knack for keeping things in perspective. Those on top have the necessary skills; those under don't.

At any rate, few who arrive at the top keep intact the

same group that they started out with. There is a necessary winnowing and pruning. Those who have the stuff to make it, make it; the rest fall away. Those that fall away are replaced by others. But those who are pruned are usually destined to feel bitter and spiteful, seeing the star as ungrateful and unappreciative of the alliances formed before reaching the top. They are also convinced they played a major role in helping the star get to the top—that the star would not have made it without them—and that they are being denied their just and well-deserved reward. It's a tough pill to swallow.

CHAPTER 28

S ome things—tastes, likes, and dislikes—don't change when celebrity wraps itself around a person. One thing that remained constant with Randy was his love of horses. Some of his fondest memories are of saddling up and riding with his family through the woods and fields around his home. And whenever he went home, he always made it a point to see Buckshot, rub him down a bit, and maybe take him out for a ride.

Though Randy always loved horses, for years he had to live without them. When he moved to Charlotte he would drive back to Marshville to ride his horses. Later he managed to find a place for Buckshot nearby, but had to send him back home to Marshville when he moved to Tennessee. Randy's life in Nashville consisted of nightclubs and Music Row offices; there was no place for a horse.

Jim Ed Norman, head of Warner Brothers' Nashville office, knew of Randy's love and decided to surprise him with a gift of a horse after the idea had been planted by publicist Evelyn Shriver. On a Sunday afternoon in late September 1987 in Red Boiling Springs, Tennessee, just before Randy's concert at the Deerwood Amphitheater in Macon County, Norman made the presentation.

Travis looked at him and asked incredulously, "You mean you're giving that to me?"

Norman nodded.

Travis looked at the horse. "Man, he is beautiful."

Norman had named the two-year-old quarter horse "Platinum Harry" in honor of the massive sales of Randy's first two albums, *Storms of Life* and *Always and Forever.* Randy's second album, which had been out four months, was number twenty-six on *Billboard*'s pop charts and number one for the thirteenth consecutive week on the country charts, with sales over three million.

Randy soon pulled Platinum Harry into a clearing. A row of trees separated the meadow from the amphitheater and three thousand of his fans. Randy stroked the horse's mane and whispered to him, then guided him in a circle, letting out the rope slowly as the circle widened.

Cameras flashed, clicked, and whirred behind him, but Randy paid no attention. Lib, who was watching, observed, "He's been riding since he was three. We had three or four horses when we were in North Carolina, but he hasn't owned one since he moved to Nashville." That meant he had been six years without a horse.

After about ten minutes, Randy reined Harry in close and started checking out some of his major features. "This is a real fine horse," he said.

Platinum Harry had come from the farm of Travis and Gail Ruffin in Ashland City, who had just purchased him a month earlier. When Norman sent word he wanted to buy a horse for Randy, Carol Harper of Randy's office arranged through Juanita Winfrey to look for one. She couldn't find any she liked and mentioned her lack of luck to Gail Ruffin. Gail thought a bit and then suggested this one.

Travis Ruffin said, "I hated to sell him. I was going to run him, but he belonged to my wife. It was her decision." He added, "That sure can be some horse if it's trained right. It can be anything he wants to make it. You don't see 'em that good too often."

From this time on, Randy would look forward to coming home off the road and riding. And after this horse, he began getting more.

CHAPTER 29

*B*y the end of 1987 Randy Travis was perhaps the best-known star of country music in the United States. In his short career he had generated more media coverage than such legends as Conway Twitty, George Jones, and Merle Haggard. How did he do it?

An important part of that answer would have to be Evelyn Shriver, the publicist he hired in August 1986.

Shriver, whose firm was based in New York, had handled clients such as Diana Ross, Alexander Godunov, Larry Hagman, and Henry Winkler. She had gotten her start as a teenage receptionist in a major New York public relations firm and worked her way up to vice president. Somewhere along the line she got tired of New York and wanted to move to Nashville.

Evelyn's goal was to give a country artist exposure outside the normal country music outlets, to get national coverage in publications whose focus was not on country music.

Her first choice as an act was Gary Morris, but she couldn't get an interview with him.

Shriver's husband, Roger, had seen Randy at the Nashville Palace and recommended him to her. Janice Azrak of Warner Brothers arranged a meeting between Randy, Lib, Evelyn, and herself at the Pancake Pantry, just off Music Row. Evelyn told them what she had in mind; Lib listened, took notice, then hired her.

Shriver was ambitious, and her strategy had several points. First, they would cover the basics—working hard on tour publicity and getting coverage in all of the towns where Randy would be performing. This meant Randy would spend hours making calls, usually from a pay phone on the side of the road, to newspaper reporters. Second, they would pursue cover stories in such specialized periodicals as *Country Music, Country Song Round-Up,* and *Music City News.* In 1987 this strategy resulted in several cover stories in those and other publications. Third, they would court other music media, such as *Rolling Stone.* Finally, they would go after print coverage in national periodicals like *USA Today, Vanity Fair, Savvy, Cosmopolitan,* and *Elle.*

In *Vogue, Harper's Bazaar, W,* and *Rolling Stone* Randy looked like a model in the illustrations accompanying the profiles. All those hours in the gym paid off. And his angular face photographed well, providing appealing pictures.

In television, the country music programs on the Nashville Network, such as "Nashville Now," gave Randy his first exposure. Soon he was on talk shows like "Tonight" and "Late Night with David Letterman" as well as the news shows "Today" and "Good Morning America." Randy's appearances on awards shows provided further television exposure.

What made the media so receptive to Randy Travis?

First, his success. Any time a first album sells a million copies, people want to know about the artist. The American consumer wants to read success stories, not stories about unknowns, and the radio and sales success of *Storms of Life* and then *Always and Forever* was a good starting point.

Next was Randy himself. He was not eaten up with being a star. Here was a guy who loved country music—shy, simple, appealing. He didn't put on airs in interviews. He was straightforward, direct, and honest. He had an interesting past—a small-town hooligan who had spent some time in the jailhouse. His boyishness and natural naïveté charmed both the fans and the press. And he was a remnant of the past—somebody who sang plain country music. He didn't merely use country music while chasing stardom; he sang country music and stardom came chasing him.

In addition, Lib Hatcher accepted every available opportunity for Randy's face and name to be known publicly. She and Randy worked hard, never refusing interviews, setting aside personal time in order to accommodate journalists and interviewers.

Finally, there was Evelyn Shriver, who used her contacts and her influence to develop a plan and make it happen. She could call reporters from the major publications and have them pay attention to her. And when she talked about Randy Travis, they listened.

Media exposure begets more media exposure, and as Randy was covered in one publication, several others wanted to do stories, too. When Evelyn said, "Better get on the bandwagon, this guy's hot," and pulled out clips to prove it, the media began a stampede to Randy Travis.

For Lib, this was the triumph of her basic philosophy. She was not afraid to spend her own money to promote Randy. So many artists leave the work of publicity to the record label's in-house publicity department. But that department is usually swamped with other acts and cannot give extra attention to an act outside the schedule of record releases. By hiring an independent publicist, Randy and Lib could receive special ongoing attention.

Lib's plan was to get as much exposure and attention for Randy as possible. She had waited a long time for this opportunity, and she wanted to make sure she capitalized on it. She thought that everybody everywhere should know who Randy Travis is and that the media was the ticket for that ride. She planned and plotted, and when she heard Evelyn Shriver say that a country artist should be getting exposure in major media in Los Angeles and New York, she hired her to carry out their dreams.

It worked like a charm.

CHAPTER *30*

*A*s Randy did more and more interviews, reporters continued to question him about his background and his early life. He was always refreshingly honest and surprisingly frank about those early years, although the intervening years had certainly helped give him a new perspective on life before stardom.

Growing up in Marshville, he said he had "never listened to much rock as a kid. It was mostly country. Hank Williams was my favorite." He added, "My dad loved country music and is very knowledgeable about it. He played Merle Haggard, Ernest Tubb, Tex Ritter, and Gene Autry. That's what I heard and what I love."

Harold Traywick is "probably the biggest country fan there ever was," he noted. "Daddy liked to sing a little bit, but not as a professional. My great-uncle and great-grandpa were also musicians, but they didn't make their careers at it."

About growing up in Marshville Randy said, "It's pretty much like most small towns—everybody knows everybody else. I was raised on a farm. Daddy had cows and horses. He had a construction business, too, and I worked in construction. I have three brothers and two sisters. I'm next to the oldest, but there's only ten years' difference from the oldest to the youngest. Seems like we were always arguing and fighting, but when you get away, you get to missing them. When you move to the city, you get to missing that kind of life. It's a good way to grow up, I think."

He also acknowledged his early troubles. "Wild? I guess you could say I was kinda wild. I got into a little trouble. I was drinking, doing a little drugs, got more parking tickets than you would believe. A lot of teenagers do that, but I was the one who got caught all the time."

Of his school life he confessed, "You're not supposed to, but I just wouldn't go. They'd say to my folks, 'He doesn't go to school.' And my folks would say, 'What can we do?' . . . I just didn't like school. After about the seventh grade I would skip school. I wound up not going more than I went, so I just decided it was better just to go ahead and quit." His parents "never said too much about it." As to the effect of quitting on his music career, "I don't know whether schooling would have helped me get farther along in music at this time. I doubt it would have. This is what I wanted to do for a long time. I wish at times I had finished school just to say I had."

Randy did have regrets about his early days. "When you're younger, you do a bunch of things, and you wonder why, or how you had the nerve, or why you were so dumb or whatever it was. I guess you grow out of it. You're lucky to live through it, I guess." He elaborated, "You go through a stage where you think you know it all and don't want nobody telling you nothing. But you get away from home and you get to missing them. I guess as you grow older, you see that they were right most of the time."

144

He noted that times have changed. "My folks and I get along great now. As I get older, I wish I could redo a lot of my mistakes." He also was pleased to see his parents' pride in his success. "They really like it, because they were the ones who pushed me to do this. Daddy was the one who bought me my first guitar, and he or Mama always made sure that me and my brother Ricky got to our guitar lessons and that we practiced. They would take us to perform different places, and Daddy took me to enter the talent contest at Lib's place. So they've been behind me the whole time."

Though Randy found pursuing a career in country music demanding, he was used to hard work. "I've done a lot of different jobs," he said. "I've been a carpenter, a painter, worked with cows and horses, even turkeys. I'm not a lazy person. I quit school at fifteen, but I've had to work hard ever since." He hated raising turkeys and thought that "being a cook is the hardest work I've ever done. I worked dinner and breakfast shifts and sometimes caught a couple hours' sleep in between. When it gets busy, it's hectic work physically, and mentally it's a strain to remember all you have to remember. I'd go home some nights more tired than when I worked in construction."

But the burning desire to sing was always there. During his Palace days, "sometimes I'd just have to whip off my white apron and go out front and sing. Whenever anybody wanted to hear me, I wanted to sing."

He said he felt that winning the talent contest at Country City USA "was my first big break. I started working for Lib and she started managing my career." He was also quick to give Lib credit for helping him straighten out his life.

About moving to Nashville he said, "I had no idea what it would be like. I had been there as a tourist and I had gone to the Opry and met people in the business like Joe Stampley and Moe Bandy. People were real nice to me. But the scene is like the radio. There's a lot of different kinds of music being played on country radio. It's not all country for sure."

He said the early frustrations never made him want to quit. "I don't know why, but I just never really got in that kind of mood. I guess I just kept saying to myself, 'One more day. One more day.'"

Being rejected in those early days turned out to be a blessing in disguise. "When I first moved to Nashville I got turned down by practically every label in town," he said. "They didn't tell me I'd never make it or anything like that—they just said they had no use for me! I think timing has a lot to do with it. It's probably for the best that they turned me down when they did, because now I'm more ready for success. I'm singing better now than I was a few years back, and mentally, I'm handling things better."

Tracing his early musical career, Randy said, "I started taking guitar lessons when I was about eight years old. When I was ten or eleven my brother and I had a little band, and we used to play around at VFW dances, square dances, and parties. I was kind of young, I know, but we were always with my mama and dad." He added, "We just had family bands; there was always some kind of band with cousins in it."

His real education consisted of singing in clubs and watching other performers. "I saw a lot of performers in my thirteen years of working in clubs. They would always be booking people from Nashville and so on in the Palace, where I worked three and a half years, and I learned a lot about how to talk to a crowd and things like that." He noted, "I've been working clubs so long, I've learned a lot of songs. With the band out there we can play and sing all night."

As for being labeled an overnight success, Randy countered, "A bunch of years went into it. I mean, I don't think anybody is really an overnight success." He reflected, "I really believe you have to wait your turn to make it in the music business. It's all in the timing. I guess it's my turn now."

Indeed, it was his turn, and he spent 1987 busier than a one-legged man at a square-dance contest. During June at Fan Fair, he performed at the International Fan Club Organization show with Conway Twitty and Loretta Lynn on Sunday night, picked up his four awards from *Music City News* on Monday night, spent Tuesday doing interviews and signing autographs at the Fan Fair booths, and did a recording session on Wednesday. That evening he attended a "catfish soiree" given by Warner Brothers in their parking lot, then left to perform as a surprise guest on the Opry Trust Fund Benefit Show. On Thursday he had his name installed in the Walkway of Stars inside the Country Music Hall of Fame, then went back to Fan Fair to sign more autographs before heading out to Music Village Theater in Hendersonville for his fan club party, organized by Lib and club president Jill Youngblood, where he performed and then signed autographs until one in the morning.

In October Randy won three awards from the Country Music Association: Male Vocalist, Best Album (for *Always and Forever*) and top single (for "Forever and Ever, Amen").

Always and Forever, his second album, had sold over two million copies and was still going strong. The first single from the album, "Forever and Ever, Amen" had stayed number one for three weeks. The second single, "Too Gone Too Long," hit number one on December 12, his seventh straight Top Ten song.

At the end of the year the American Music Operators Association, who give awards for jukebox play, gave "Forever and Ever, Amen" the top country award. That meant that a lot of quarters dropped down the slot while this number was pressed.

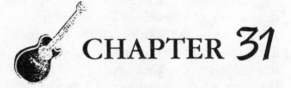

CHAPTER 31

By 1988 Randy Travis was looking for new worlds to conquer. Safely ensconced at the top of the country music world, this year he branched out, appearing on major network television programs, touring Europe and the Far East, and appearing in major venues as a headliner.

On June 11 "I Told You So" became his first original song to reach number one. And in what was now becoming a habit, Randy continued winning awards.

At the Fifteenth Annual American Music Awards on January 26 he won every award he was nominated for: Favorite Country LP for *Always and Forever* as well as Favorite Country Single and Favorite Country Video for "Forever and Ever, Amen," which he also performed on the show. On March 2 he won his first Grammy, for Country Male Vocalist, saying afterward, "There is no way to describe how it feels to win a Grammy. It's something you dream about, and it's hard for it to sink in once it happens. It will be something I'll always cherish and remember. But you have to understand that we have some real good people writing for us and working with us to help make these awards and record sales happen. Our songwriters have produced amazing songs, and we have been fortunate to have them writing for us. I owe a great deal to a lot of people: my family, my songwriters, my agent, my support people, my record producers, and especially my fans."

During the Viewer's Choice Awards from TNN in April Randy won Performer of the Year, Favorite Male Performer, Album of the Year (for *Always and Forever*), and Favorite Video (for "Forever and Ever, Amen") while the Favorite Song award went to songwriters Paul Overstreet and Don Schlitz for "Forever and Ever, Amen." These awards came from about 318,000 TNN viewers, who chose the winners by telephone balloting between February 8 and April 3. By this time the Nashville Network was reaching forty million households.

At the *Music City News* Awards on June 6 Randy dominated, dethroning the Statler Brothers, who, along with Barbara Mandrell, hosted the show. Prizes went to Randy, "Forever and Ever, Amen" (both video and single), and *Always and Forever.* Randy also won the top prize: Entertainer of the Year, triumphing over Reba McEntire, the Statlers, George Strait, and Hank Williams, Jr.

Discussing awards shows, Randy told Vincent Creel of the Biloxi-Gulfport *Sun Herald,* "I don't know exactly why it is. When you win something you, of course, have to get up and go accept the award. You want to say something good, as everybody would want to. That just makes me nervous. Awards shows make me more nervous than any type of show I've ever done."

About winning awards and achieving the kind of success he was achieving Randy said to another reporter, "That sort of reception is something you never get used to. I've never really planned ahead all that much. I've never thought, 'Well, I want to accomplish this and this.' I don't look at my career like that. It's not like I'm setting goals for myself. I've never done that."

Still, after carrying home awards of every type and size, Randy reiterated that "of all the awards, I guess the one that means the most to me is being inducted into the Grand Ole Opry. The Opry has always been a symbol of country music. The real big names and pioneers of country music performed there and made it what it is. I love country music, and used to listen to the Opry on the radio just to hear my favorites perform. It is all I could ever ask for to walk backstage, have some of the country music idols speak to me, and call me by name like I'm a member of the family. It is a dream come true for a small-town country boy from Marshville, North Carolina."

Randy made his first major appearance in New York on Saturday, May 21, 1988, at Madison Square Garden as part of the 1988 Marlboro Country Music Tour. He opened the show, and was followed by the Judds, George Strait, and the show's closer, Alabama.

New York Times reviewer Stephen Holden wrote, "An artistic disciple of Merle Haggard and George Jones, the masters of a twangy vocal whine that evokes a rock-bottom pathos along with an earthy realism, Mr. Travis is like an eerie voice out of the past. . . . He imbues every lyric with an aura of deep, serious nostalgia for a picture-perfect rustic never-never land of social and romantic harmony." Randy exuded a quality that "suggested a preternaturally wise child expressing the kind of weathered fatalism that would normally be the province of singers twenty or more years older than he is."

He had appeared on "Saturday Night Live" in April and commented, "That one was a lot more foreign to me than I must have been to them. I felt a little out of place to start with because the show mainly deals with rock and roll, as far as music goes. But I couldn't have asked to be treated any better."

He had spent a full day rehearsing with host Tom Hanks. The two had recorded a promotional spot for the show that Randy was clearly excited about. "I say, 'I'm a pickin',' and Tom says, 'I'm a grinnin',' with this real silly smile on his face, just like the old 'Hee Haw' things. It's pretty nice."

But the small-town boy had some reservations about the Big Apple. When asked about his reaction to New York City, Randy answered, "Well . . . I've enjoyed visiting here, but it's a little too . . . busy for me. I couldn't live here. Last year, we were coming out of the NBC building when they were lighting the Christmas tree at Rockefeller Center, and it was a real mess. I was with Lib and Evelyn, and there was such a crowd of people, we had to hold hands to keep from getting separated. That's too busy for me."

Randy was staying busy, settling into a lifestyle of constant travel and performing on the road. He had done over two hundred concerts in 1987; he would do a little more in 1988, even though at the end of each year he would express the hope that he could cut back on road appearances and stay home more. But that was one wish that would not come true for him.

He was getting regular coverage in the media. In a profile in the *Los Angeles Times* magazine, noted writer and music critic Robert Hilburn stated, "Randy Travis is the most dramatic success story in country music in a decade. When people around town are asked to suggest someone with a similar impact on audiences, they whisper such names as Elvis and Patsy Cline. . . . His music is so pure country that pop stations don't play it. Most pop fans probably know him better from his appearances on TV awards shows than for his string of country hits." Travis is "a man of few words. There is no sense of pretense or false intimacy about him."

Playgirl listed him as one of the sexiest men in country music. *USA Today* printed the list, prompting a local Nashville radio station to conduct its own poll. The only artist who landed on both lists was Randy Travis.

On June 8 Randy and his entourage left for a twelve-day tour of Europe that would include performances in London, Paris, Dublin, and Amsterdam. Before he left he confessed, "I'm a little nervous. I'm not sure what the response will be." After he returned he admitted the tour "was an odd situation. Only a couple of my records get airplay on stations over there. It was like starting over. But a lot of people had the albums, like *Always and Forever.* And in a couple of places they knew a lot of the songs. They were small crowds, but they were receptive."

At his concert in London's Albert Hall, Mick Jagger and Jerry Hall were in the audience. After the concert Mick and Jerry invited Randy and Lib out to dinner, but because of crowded schedules they were unable to oblige.

This was not the first time Randy had performed abroad, but it was the first time he had played before native audiences. In December 1987 he had performed for thirty thousand American troops on a USO Christmas tour of military bases in Italy and Germany. With him on the tour were the McCarters.

Randy's third album, *Old 8 × 10,* was released June 30. It was originally scheduled for July 12, but the release was moved up to make it eligible for the CMA awards on October 10. Some of the LPs were pressed offcenter, however, and had to be recalled. There was an initial order of 900,000 copies—just short of platinum—placed by stores.

Old 8 × 10 begins with the bluesy "Honky Tonk Moon" and its vivid evocation of a relaxed evening in the country. In "Deeper Than the Holler" Paul Overstreet and Don Schlitz provide some fresh country imagery to counter tired pop-song clichés about the heights and depths of love.

"It's Out of My Hands" is one of the two songs on the album co-written by Randy with John Lindley. It is a stone country ballad about a love that's finished but Randy's songs hint at a musical sophistication with their use of an occasional minor chord to give a subtle update of the standard three-chord country song.

The bluegrass instrumentation and lively pace of "Is It Still Over?," written by Ken Bell and Larry Henley, provide a sparkling setting of such humorous lines as "Since my phone still ain't ringing I assume it still ain't you."

"Old 8 × 10" is another country ballad and Randy shows an impressive vocal range, keeping a resonant quality in his voice as it ranges over an octave.

"Written in Stone," a witty declaration of love by Don Schlitz and Mac McAnally, leads into the harmonically sophisticated "The Blues in Black and White," with clarinets lending their distinctive color. "Here in My Heart" is a bluesy waltz that opens with a simple accompaniment of fiddle and acoustic guitar. Gene Pistilli and Larry Henley's western-swing "We Ain't Out of Love Yet" offers sound advice for troubled love: "we don't need a lawyer, we just need a rest."

"Promises," which Randy co-wrote with John Lindley, is reprised from the Nashville Palace album. Randy sings it here with just his own guitar accompaniment and a discreet vocal backing in places, and the result is stunning. With nothing to distract, the listener focuses on Randy's resonant baritone. Though Randy doesn't consider himself a vocal technician, it's evident here that his expressive range and subtle phrasing put him in the same league with the greatest country singers.

During his concert at Starwood Amphitheater in Nashville on June 25, according to critic Robert Oermann, "women flowed down to the stage in a steady stream offering him flowers throughout the first few songs. Screams greeted almost every song, whether a radio staple or not."

Oermann also observed that "the twenty-nine-year-old new Nashville sensation still seems a little frightened by his stardom. He looks more boyish and fragile than ever, and his overwhelming concert load has cast an almost wan reflection on his face. The restrained melancholy in his voice gives each performance extra poignancy. Every now and then a shy smile breaks across his stony expression."

 CHAPTER 32

When he first rose to fame, Randy was asked a lot of questions about his past. As he looked at the industry from his lofty perch on top of the country music empire, he began to be asked questions about his future as well as the future of country music.

From his earliest successes, Randy sensed there would come a time when things would not be this good, when not all the records would turn gold and not all the crowds would fill large auditoriums, clamoring to see him.

In the early days, as the phone calls came in to book personal appearances, he told Martin Grosswendt of the Providence *Bulletin,* "We're very fortunate to have steady work, because I know that'll slow down sooner or later. That's just the nature of the business.

He seemed to accept the notion that one day all the success will somehow fade away, commenting to Robert Hilburn that "I know that has to happen. . . . I'm just gonna

155

keep doing what we're doing. We don't plan that far ahead. We just kinda take things as they come, deal with them, and do the best we can at what we're doing."

He confessed that "really, all I ever wanted was to be able to make music and earn a living doing it. I realize this may not last forever. That's why I'm working all the time—touring, writing. I want to take advantage of my good fortune and make the most of it."

He philosophized to Tommy Goldsmith of the Nashville *Tennessean* that someday his time will be over. "I'm sure it will. It happens to everybody. You have to have a beginning, go up, and hopefully ride that for a while. The nature of the business is that you'll go back down. Hopefully, you will be able to go back down and maintain that for a while like Conway Twitty has done. He's maintained for a lot of years."

He also admitted, "I'm not one that sits and thinks about all that a lot, anyway. I just kind of take it as it comes. I've never been one to plan ahead and say I want to accomplish this by such and such a date. I know that it can't continue. I know that sooner or later it's going to slow down whether I want it to or not. So I'm just enjoying it while it happens."

Money was a concern. "Ten years down the road, when things aren't going like they are now—and I know they won't—I want to be able to think that I'm financially all right."

When asked about his success, Randy has been unable to explain it. He told Barbara Jaeger of the Hackensack *Record,* "I don't think too much about what has happened, but when I do, I get kind of overwhelmed."

To another reporter he said, "I don't know what else we could wish for. These past two years have been unbelievable, you know—so unexpected. The kind of music that we do hasn't been known to sell a lot of records over the past few years or draw a lot of people to shows. It's been real shocking. We've been lucky. We've had some quality songs that some people don't get their whole careers. I don't know why we've been so lucky in that respect." He revealed that his rise to the top "has been scary at times," but sensed that his years struggling in Nashville had paid off. "I guess the fact that I'd been around the business so much and knew a lot about the business before anything ever happened made it easier to deal with, 'cause I pretty much knew what has to be done."

Looking back at 1987 he mused, "The whole year has gone by in a flash."

He always admitted he enjoyed the success and hoped it would continue. It had brought some changes in his life, he told Mark Fair of the Akron *Beacon Journal.* "I eat a little better these days—a little more, too. I guess I dress a little better and I have maybe more confidence in what I do on stage. I've grown a little more tired of the business end of the business and all the extra demands on my time that take away from the music. But overall, I haven't really changed. Me and the band and the crew still travel together on the bus. We play cards, joke around, work on songs—you know, enjoy what we're doing. Yeah, I'm pretty much the same guy I've always been."

He wanted to take advantage of the demand. "I'm not slowing down, not now. I'll always sing, but not at the pace I'm doing it now."

Still, there were some things he did not like about his newfound stardom. He told Robert Ross of the Hershey *Patriot,* "Being gone most of the time is the only thing I don't like. I enjoy doing the live shows a lot, but I enjoy being home a little more than that."

When asked what was left for him to accomplish he told one reporter, "I'm pretty simple as far as that goes. I was raised on a farm in North Carolina, and at some point I'd like to have a farm with pasture land and run horses on it, maybe cows, too. I really like that kind of living."

Trying to explain why so many young people are coming to his shows and listening to traditional country music, he admitted to a reporter, "It's just been shocking . . . hard to believe. I've been trying to figure out just what turned the younger people on to the real country music. I think maybe Alabama and Hank Williams, Jr., who do some rock, helped me in a way. I think maybe young people raised on rock heard Alabama and Hank, Jr., on the rock stations and heard them later on a country station and just happened to stay tuned and hear country. Of course, it sure ain't hard for me to understand why anybody'd love the good real country once they heard it."

To another reporter he said, "I didn't expect the kids to come to my shows. I wondered where they had heard the songs. The best explanation I can find is that they heard them from their moms and dads. And in our case, a lot of people come to the shows who say they're not country fans, but they like us and Strait. I don't have a great explanation."

When asked why he thought some singers who found success in traditional country insisted on branching into pop or rock, he surmised, "I figure their only reason for doing something like that was because they didn't really love country in the first place. They probably saw it only as a chance to get where they wanted to go. One thing for sure—what I'm doing is working and I always believed if something ain't broke, don't go fixing it."

He had made no pretenses about his own music. "What we are doing is definitely rooted in the past. Most of the songs on my albums could have been cut fifteen or twenty years ago by Hank or Lefty or George Jones, and I wondered for a while if that kind of music was going to disappear."

Randy admitted to wanting stardom, but also that he never had any grand plan to get it. He told Robert Hilburn, "Sometimes when I sit and think about it, it really seems hard to believe. . . . None of this was ever a [strategy]. It was what I was singing from the first day I was singing. I can honestly say I never tried to make believe that I am something I am not."

And he asserted to another reporter that he still loved to sing. "Just about every evening I sit out there on the bus and sing some songs."

As for the future, Randy said to Carrie Maynard of the Reuters News Service in 1988, "There's not much that I would wish for that hasn't happened. I love to entertain. Even if I live to be seventy or eighty, I'll still want to sing." He paused, then laughed, "'Course, I don't know by then if anyone will want to hear it."

But to Robert Oermann he confessed, "Actually, I do want to slow down a bit, somewhere down the line. But it seems there's always something to do in the business."

CHAPTER 33

O n Randy's twenty-ninth birthday Lib gave him two new horses—Red Star Cause, a high sorrel quarter horse, and Smokey's Red Rouge, a tan and white Appaloosa. The horses, which were presented to Randy with big bows around their necks, would keep Platinum Harry company. Randy was acquiring quite a stable at his farm near Ashland City.

This birthday had been celebrated with a party at Lib and Randy's office on Sixteenth Avenue with a Mexican luncheon. Randy's parents and his youngest brother, Dennis, came over from Marshville as a special surprise.

Randy debuted some of the songs from his *Old 8 × 10* album before his fan club during the June 1988 Fan Fair. The club's dinner attracted twelve hundred people to the Nashville Convention Center on the evening before Randy and his entourage were set to leave for Europe. The show was emceed by Jeff Davis, vice president of Special Moments

Promotions, the concert booking firm that Lib and Randy had begun, and fan club president Jill Youngblood. After dinner, Randy's band performed a short acoustic set. New member Monty Parkie replaced Drew Sexton, who had elected to move back to his home in Oneida, Tennessee. Then Randy came up and performed his set. Afterward he signed autographs for five hours—until 2 A.M.—writing his name on pictures, scraps of paper, albums, and just about anything else his fans brought to sign.

There is a genuine love, a feeling of "family," between Randy and his fans. It is ironic (or perhaps appropriate) that in a time when the concept of family is falling apart and family values seem to be disintegrating, the country music community refers to itself as a family. And in a sense it is, bound by a kinship to a cause and pulling together in times of crises. There are family squabbles, gossip, and backbiting—even some incest.

When Randy returned from his European tour, Warner Brothers threw a massive bash to celebrate the fact that his first albums had sold over five million copies. The party, whose theme was "Working Out with Randy Travis," was held at the West Side Athletic Club in Nashville, with refreshments like fresh fruit and juices, seafood, and non-alcoholic beverages. Some professional hunks provided the entertainment, demonstrating lifting exercises and showing off their physiques. The music industry loves to party and loves honoring itself. Randy's success was giving it ample opportunities for both.

By the end of 1988 Randy had finally become comfortable with his stardom, accepting himself as a major star in country music and easily handling all the different situations a celebrity must deal with.

On tour in California at the end of the summer, Randy spent a day with Roy Rogers. They quickly became friends and made plans to record "Happy Trails" together in January for an album of duets that Randy wanted to put together. Later, Roy agreed to come to the Country Music Association's awards show if he could be seated next to Randy. When the show rolled around in October Randy won the Male Vocalist crown again and experienced the thrill of having host Dolly Parton sit in his lap.

At the end of the year, in what had become a tradition, Randy headed north to Alaska with the USO on November 29 to perform for the troops, then traveled on to Japan and Korea.

The media spotlight stayed fixed on Randy. He appeared with Special Olympics children on "A Very Special Christmas Party," broadcast on December 22 over the ABC network, and was the subject of an "At Home" profile on "Entertainment Tonight." He also appeared on the cover of a men's fitness magazine, *Men's Health,* as well as on the covers of the *Saturday Evening Post* and *Glamour.* In a Gallup poll surveying teenagers for their favorite male artists, Randy came in fifth, behind George Michael, Bon Jovi, Bono, and Michael Jackson.

He closed the year at Bally's in Las Vegas on New Year's Eve, then headed out to Los Angeles, where he performed on an American Cinema Awards salute to Clint Eastwood. He was walking in high cotton, and professionally things were looking rosy.

But there were problems as well. Jill Youngblood was in Ohio being treated for cancer. Lib and Randy had known Jill since the Charlotte days, when she had a record shop in Country City USA and had started Randy's fan club in 1984. She had moved to Nashville earlier in 1988 to be closer to Lib and Randy and to the country music scene. Lib liked the idea of Jill living in Nashville—they were close friends—and thought it would be more efficient for Jill to run the club, which had grown so large that it was getting hard to handle, out of their office.

CHAPTER 34

*T*here have long been whispers about the relationship between Randy and his manager, Lib Hatcher. Even those who have traveled with them can only guess about what goes on behind closed doors. The two constantly deny the rumors of a secret marriage that have circulated since they first came into the spotlight. The rumors and innuendos have been around since the Charlotte days, exacerbated by the fact that Lib chose Randy instead of her husband when the marital showdown occurred.

Back at the end of 1985, when Randy was on Ralph Emery's "Nashville Now," a call-in questioner asked him, "Are you married? Do you want to be?"

Randy answered that he was not married, but as for wanting to be, "I don't know. I haven't given it much thought."

When Emery learned Randy was twenty-six he said, "You're getting to be eligible."

Randy replied, "I guess. I don't know how old you have to be to be eligible."

Ralph then asked if there was a serious romance in his life, and Randy replied, "Well, sometimes."

Randy has told interviewers, "Someday I would love to get married. I'll make the time some day. Right now, I don't even have a steady girlfriend." To another interviewer he has confessed, "I don't really have much of a personal life at the moment, being so far from home as I am so much of the time." He and Lib are "very close friends. We've been working together for so long we really care what happens to each other."

But as time continues to pass and more and more reporters press Randy about his relationship with Lib, he seems at times to get a little testy, emphatically denying a romantic relationship, saying, "It's a business relationship, but we also are good friends. There's no romantic involvement."

He acknowledges their tremendous closeness and the debt he owes her for guiding his career. "I was lucky to have met her. Anybody's lucky when they meet somebody they can trust completely. Of course, we have our differences, but we always work them out. I've never met anybody that works as hard as she does."

Responding to a question about friction between the two, he says, "I don't think that's going to happen to us. I know that when a lot of people get successful they get greedy, but we work together and we listen to each other. We plan to stay together."

He told one reporter, "I've learned a lot from my manager, Lib Hatcher. We've been working together for over ten years now. As far as the music business goes, we both learned as we went, to tell you the truth. She had no experience in managing a person or managing a career, but she's a smart enough person to know right from wrong and to learn as she went, and that's pretty much what we've both done. I feel lucky to have had somebody who is that smart and somebody that cared enough in life to work as hard for me as she has. Not everybody is lucky enough in life to have somebody to work for them that much and to care that much about what they do. . . . I don't know if I would have made it without her. I'm not good at pushing myself on people, I guess, is the thing. She'll do that for me. I trust her completely."

Responding to questions about their relationship, Lib has said, "We trust each other and really care about each other's feelings." Regarding marriage, "there are no plans."

She admits to hearing the rumors; Tammy Wynette had even called to congratulate her on getting married. "But I don't worry about it. People don't understand how people can be this close . . . how we can be best friends." She has stated to associates that one marriage was enough, and told her father, who asked if she and Randy were married, "Who has time?"

She has admitted to others, "I think there's trust there that you can't put into words. We're best friends." To one reporter who insisted on knowing their relationship Lib replied, "I'm his manager. I'm not his girlfriend, not his wife, not his mother. I'm his best friend."

Lib can be domineering, and wryly noted to one reporter, "We see things the same way. My way."

Randy has said that he has "never been that serious about anybody. Guess I haven't met the right person yet." Nobody in Marshville can ever recall Randy having a girlfriend or going out with girls. His Marshville days were filled with going out with the boys, drinking, and raising hell. And even those who knew him in Charlotte or the early days of Nashville can not recall his having girlfriends or dates—just Lib as a constant companion.

Randy and Lib are always together at public functions, but they never show affection for each other in public. They have lived under the same roof since 1977 and traveled together all over the world, and Lib has never missed a performance by Randy.

A lot of people speculate about whether Randy and Lib are sleeping together. When people from Marshville who know Randy talk about him they always openly wonder if he's married Lib yet. But Randy has made it clear that they have a business relationship, and while Lib tends to be more vague, neither admits to a romance that will lead to marriage.

In the end, they should be allowed their private lives. What does it matter, really, to anyone but them? The people who are most concerned with the question tend to be interested in gossip, not genuinely concerned about either Randy Travis or Lib Hatcher.

But surrounding each superstar is a maelstrom of gossip, and rumors about Randy and Lib are bound to continue. One thing is certain: the bond between these two transcends all the rumors and gossip. Their deep respect and trust for each other date back to Charlotte and 1977, when Randy was a wild kid heading down the wrong road and Lib was the person who became the principal catalyst not only for turning his personal life around, but also for his becoming the biggest country music star of the 1980s.

CHAPTER 35

*R*andy and pop star George Michael swept the American Music Awards on January 30, 1989, winning three each. Randy's awards came for Favorite Male Vocalist, Album (*Always and Forever*), and Single ("I Told You So").

He made the news in other ways as well. On January 17 he was in a traffic accident in Cheatham County, ending up in a ditch while trying to avoid another car. Randy and Lib were on their way to a local high school to promote a new booklet on teenage problems. He had been named honorary chairman of the *Youth Yellow Pages,* a directory of information and telephone numbers for teenagers concerned about AIDS, alcohol, drugs, peer pressure, pregnancy, sexual abuse, venereal disease, and violence.

The accident didn't stop him from an appearance on "Late Night with David Letterman" or singing on Thursday night at President Bush's inaugural gala, but it did remind Lib that she still didn't like Randy's driving. She had always said he drove too fast.

* * *

At the Grammys, held Wednesday, February 22, 1989, in Los Angeles, Randy won his second Grammy, this one for *Old 8 × 10.*

"I'm glad I came," Randy told the crowd. Backstage he admitted to the press, "Believe it or not, I didn't even fill in my form [ballot]. Lib did it for me. She might have voted for me."

Other country Grammies went to Bill Monroe, the Judds, K. T. Oslin, the duet of Roy Orbison and k. d. lang, and Asleep at the Wheel. But the evening belonged to Bobby McFerrin and Tracy Chapman. Randy had served, along with pop star and Nashville resident Steve Winwood, in presenting Chapman with one of her awards. Hosted by Billy Crystal, the Grammys featured country performances by K. T. Oslin, Lyle Lovett, and the duet of Buck Owens and Dwight Yoakam.

While in Los Angeles Randy accepted an invitation from Arnold Schwarzenegger for a seven A.M. workout. He was surprised to see the bodybuilder go quickly from one exercise to the next without stopping. After the workout Randy and Lib had lunch with Arnold and his wife, TV newscaster Maria Shriver. Maria told Randy that country music was all Arnold listened to.

As winter turned to spring the awards kept coming. He was voted Favorite Male Vocalist over George Michael and Michael Jackson at the People's Choice Awards in Los Angeles. On April 25 he took home his second Entertainer of the Year and Best Album awards from TNN's Viewer's Choice Awards.

On Randy's thirtieth birthday he was playing a concert in Sydney, Nova Scotia. Onstage the band kicked off "Happy Birthday," and Randy was caught by surprise. Then a birthday video was shown for him with greetings from folks like Roy Acuff, Minnie Pearl, Ricky Van Shelton, Reba McEntire,

Highway 101, Buck Owens, Dwight Yoakam, and Ralph Emery.

Being on the road had now become an accepted way of life for Randy. It seemed like he was always climbing aboard a bus or plane heading out for somewhere. It had gotten to the point where he slept better on the bus than he did at home—the hum of the motor was a lullaby. At home he found he had to turn on a fan for some noise before he could get to sleep. The silence was just too deafening. The way his life was going Randy might end up like Ernest Tubb, who had grown so accustomed to sleeping on his big tour bus that when he was home he kept it parked outside his house. When he was ready to go to sleep, the Texas Troubadour would go out to the bus, turn on the motor, and crawl into his bed in the back.

Randy's gift shop opened in Nashville on May 11, in time for Fan Fair visitors to buy some goodies. The whole display area would not be open until August, featuring a room dedicated to fans, with the old bread truck he used on his early tours on display. The walls there are covered with gifts fans have made for him as well as notes from fans.

CHAPTER 36

*R*andy Travis steps into the spotlight and sings for an hour or so. His fans scream and applaud—he is loved. The people who come to see him are hardworking, and it isn't always easy for them to pay fifteen or twenty dollars a ticket, not to mention making all the necessary arrangements to get there and putting up with parking and the crowd. Some fans are able to put down some more of their money for T-shirts, sweatshirts, hats, or tapes.

Those people attending the concert make twenty to thirty thousand dollars a year; some make more, many less. Randy might make over $100,000 just this evening for singing.

Tomorrow the fans will go back to their workaday world, to jobs that take their time and body and seldom pay them what they're worth, or to bosses who seldom show any real appreciation. Meanwhile Randy's records are selling in the stores, his songs are on the radio, his picture is all over the front pages, and he's raking in so much dough he needs a shovel to keep the front door clear. And tomorrow night, when these fans are plopped in front of the tube, Randy's gonna be singing somewhere else, making another $100,000 for his hour or so.

Some people have all the luck and none of the hassles, say the fans. But there's a lot more to it.

After the concert, you're tired, but there's a reporter with some questions before the bus pulls out. And there are important people to meet backstage, hands to shake, pictures to take, autographs to sign.

You get on board your bus and head to another town. You don't remember the name of the town you just played and aren't sure where you're going next. There are business decisions to think about. And the bed you're lying in is moving down the highway about sixty-five miles an hour. It would be nice to look out the window and see the same scenery two days in a row.

At the next stop there are things to do, more interviews where the same questions are asked over and over. How many times can a person answer those questions in a different way? You begin to hear yourself answering them in your sleep. Whenever you see another reporter coming, you don't even want to wait for the question—you just open your mouth and let the same answers come out. You don't even have to think about it anymore.

The concerts themselves have become a routine of singing. The same songs night after night. Your mind is drifting away because it all comes out automatically. You're sick of doing the same songs, but you still have to do them because those fans paid good money to hear them, and they would rightfully be hostile if you didn't do them just like the record. You've sung those songs 250 times this year and 250 times the year before and the year before that, and when you look ahead, you hear yourself singing them 250 times a

year for the rest of your life. It makes you seriously con-
template early retirement.

The money's great, but there's no time to really enjoy it. If
you buy a farm you can never be there to enjoy yourself,
because you have to be out playing more gigs. You have to
hire more people to keep the organization running, and that
means you're responsible for whole families. So you have to
work even more. And you have to buy bigger and better
equipment, and buses and tractor-trailer rigs to haul it all
down the road. And then you have to work more to pay for
them. There's the IRS to pay, as well as a whole battery of
lawyers, accountants, financial advisors, and others you need
even though you're not always sure you trust them.

The pressure alone is enough to blow the top off Mount
Saint Helens again. Everybody wants something: your
money—for an investment or just to give away—or your
time, which becomes even more valuable because you're
already giving it to everybody else and you don't have
nearly enough for yourself.

You're in this pressure cooker, but you can't just throw
up your hands, say, "I quit," and walk away. There are too
many obligations and responsibilities. There are contracts
telling you where you have to be years from now. And your
overhead has grown to astronomical proportions. You get to
the point that you have to have six thousand people come
to a concert just to break even.

And even if you did quit, you couldn't escape your fame.
You couldn't walk around in K-Mart like everybody else on
a Saturday. You would still have to put up with people pushing and shoving and asking for autographs and pictures and
favors wherever you go. And who wants to just sit in a room
hiding his whole life? Look what happened to Elvis.

Whatever happens to you—especially the bad things—is
public knowledge, spread all over the newsstands. A fan can
go out some night and get a little crazy, and all he has the

next day is a hangover. You do that and you're front-page news.

Even the reviews aren't always going to be great. In the second half of 1988 Randy performed two concerts and got raked. A reviewer in Santa Ana, California, said of his concert at the Pacific Amphitheater, "Travis barely moved on stage, and his talk was limited to charming but stiff song introductions and a couple of terrible jokes that could have come right out of some send-away volume called 'Sure Fire Laffs.' He's been telling one of these jokes for at least the last two years, and one suspects that we'll be hearing this one on tours to come until he memorizes another one."

And a reviewer in Wallingford, Connecticut, wrote, "I have three words to describe Randy Travis in concert: boring, boring, boring. While this silver-tongued cowboy may sound good on record, in concert Randy Travis has less charisma than Michael Dukakis.

"If you can't resist the concert urge, pick up one of his records, play it on an old stereo with a warped needle, stare at his cute photo on the cover, and eat a piece of Wonder Bread. What you'll experience and remember is quite similar to a Randy Travis concert: good music marred by poor reproduction, someone cute to look at, and an overall bland taste."

Even some fans were getting upset with Randy. One irate fan wrote a letter to *Country Music USA* magazine complaining that he had attended two concerts "and neither time did [Randy] take the time to talk to the fans or sign autographs." This fan blamed Lib and asserted, "It seems to me he should need his fans a lot more than his manager." Lib "may have gotten him to the stage and recording studios, but the fans bought the albums and tickets to the show."

This fan saw a fourteen-year-old girl crying "because he didn't have the time to sign her album after she waited an hour and was told that he would." He concluded, "It's a shame that anyone that good could be ruined because of bad management or a jealous manager. To me that is a waste of talent and considerably unfair to country music lovers, not to mention Randy himself. I have met Randy in person, and he is very kind, sweet, and willing to talk to people, but in the middle of our conversation he was jerked away and pushed on the bus by his manager. I assure you he was not harmed in any way. I found her rudeness completely un-called for. I know they have a fifty-fifty business arrange-ment, but I wonder if that includes his living, breathing, thinking, and personal opinions, too. . . . Can he go to the bathroom without permission?"

Publicist Evelyn Shriver responded to that letter in the following issue. "There is not a day that goes by that Randy does not sign at least a hundred and fifty autographs." She continued that Randy "is lucky if he has two or three days a month when he doesn't have to either do interviews, meet fans, perform a concert, record a song, or in some way be the 'public' Randy Travis. Consider what it might be like to be always on display. The tour bus is your home, and people are always knocking on it, peering in the windows, rushing onto it if the door is left unlocked and a security person is not posted outside." If Lib or someone else "doesn't protect Randy from himself and his availability, the very thing the fans love—his voice and the music—would be ruined. Randy suffers from an allergy to dust, and the summer fairs nearly kill his voice. He tries to preserve his voice as much as possible and doesn't even talk to the people that travel with him. When Lib Hatcher rushes Randy onto the bus it is for his own good and the good of his fans." Evelyn con-cluded, "It's a very difficult situation to try and make every-one happy. Ultimately a performer's responsibility is to deliver the product that a fan pays for, and that is a great show and a great record. The music is what they spend their money on, and I doubt you'll find many people that have been disappointed by Randy in that department."

There isn't enough money in the world to put up with all this aggravation. But money isn't the reason you got into it in the first place. The reason is the music. That's what people don't understand. They all see big dollar signs and think that's everything in the world. But it's the music that's everything. And the biggest pain is that the music itself is stuck in a rut, and the bigger the hits, the deeper the ruts.

Still, when you weigh it all you'd rather be doing this than anything else. The fans who trudge to jobs they hate know this, and that's where the real envy lies. So you keep on singing even when it's all driving you crazy because that hour or so on stage is the only time you've got to yourself, when you can do what you do and be who you are.

CHAPTER 37

*J*une in Nashville means Fan Fair. And Fan fair means over twenty thousand country music fans from all over the country coming to Music City USA to see the stars, gather memorabilia, collect autographs, visit with other fans, watch special performances, and visit the booths where artists and fans come together.

Fan Fair 1989 began with the *Music City News* Awards, held Monday, June 5. It was a night full of glitter and gleam as the TV cameras rolled on the stage of the Grand Ole Opry House, a night when country fans were in heaven, surrounded by the stars.

The stars themselves dress to the nines, while others dress to look like stars. Sometimes it's hard to tell who is what. The show is a little different from most awards shows, which are packed with industry insiders much too cool and callous to be very emotional about any act or performance. At the Music City News Awards is an abundance of fans who are downright proud to be demonstrative when their favorite singers are around. There's plenty of yelping and cheering and flashbulbs popping and requests for autographs.

When Randy and Lib came out from backstage to take their seats just before the show began, huge cheers went up from the fans, and female voices yelled, "Randy," trying to get his attention. During the commercial breaks in the show, fans yelled out Randy's name, hoping he would acknowledge them, and squealed with delight when he turned and looked their way.

The two-hour show, hosted by Barbara, Louise, and Irlene Mandrell, featured performances by Ray Stevens, Conway Twitty, Ricky Van Shelton, the Mandrell Sisters, Kathy Mattea, the Statler Brothers, and Randy, who sat on a stool at the edge of the stage with just his guitar and sang "Promises."

Most of the evening belonged to Ricky Van Shelton, who won awards for male artist, single, album, and video of the year. But he acknowledged his old friend when, accepting his second award, he looked over and said, "Randy Travis, I know how you feel tonight!"

Randy sat in the audience most of the evening, hearing his name called as a nominee but not as a winner. After his performance, near the end of the show, he stayed backstage while George Jones announced the nominees for Entertainer of the Year. Then George tore open the envelope and read the winner: Randy Travis.

Randy came out smiling and confessed, "I was beginning to get worried." Looking at George Jones, he said, "It couldn't be given to me by anybody that I would like more than this man here," acknowledging the legendary singer as one of his heroes. It was the second consecutive year for Randy to win this award.

He smiled and laughed and talked some more, holding his trophy high while the fans continued to scream and applaud. Then he went backstage, where he reflected, "I've been lucky to win what I have; I've always said I know the time will come when I won't win. Just be thankful for what you have. And I've had plenty."

But the strain of touring was telling on Randy, who would soon leave for Australia. He seemed a bit pale and tired and had been nursing a severe throat infection the past few days. He admitted, "I would like to slow down just a little bit. It's just too hard on you, too hard on your throat."

On Tuesday morning, June 6, Randy was at the Tennessee State Fairgrounds signing autographs at the Warner Brothers booth. The line of fans waiting for an autograph and a few moments with the young singer wound around the whole building—well over one hundred yards. Some fans had been there since five A.M.

Meanwhile Randy smiled, signed autographs, and posed for pictures as the security guards kept the line moving. Finally he had to leave, and the fans shrieked with displeasure—there were hundreds of people still in line. But it would have taken the entire day to sign something for everybody. So, surrounded by police, wedged in tight so that he could hardly move, Randy left the booth and exited the building while some fans openly cried.

At three that afternoon he was in his fan club's booth, signing more autographs. The line had begun forming while Randy was in the Warner Brothers booth five hours earlier. The area was so packed you could not move. The police came and tried unsuccessfully to organize the crowd into an orderly line. The fans wanted a picture because an autograph was probably out of the question. "He ain't gonna sign, anyway," one woman yelled, and the rest agreed.

There were no hard feelings; it was obvious that signing autographs for this many people was impossible. But they weren't going to get cheated out of the next best thing—a picture of their favorite.

Why do these people love Randy Travis so much? "I like

his singing," said one woman. Another said, "'Cause he's just a down-to-earth country person like I was raised," while another answered, "He's just sweet. And I love his songs."

But whatever the reason, it was obvious that Randy Travis had touched each of their lives in a special way, just as his voice and his songs speak to people every day in their homes, over the radio and through stereo speakers. He's not just Randy Traywick anymore, answering only to himself or to a few people around him; he is Randy Travis and he belongs to the world. And that world makes demands of him that he cannot deny. He must be seen and touched as well as heard when he sings.

People who are total strangers to him know him intimately. They know his likes, dislikes, hobbies, songs. And somehow they feel that he knows them too, because his music has touched them, his songs have spoken to them, his life means something to them. It is hard for them to grasp that the Randy Travis they know so well might not be the Randy Travis living inside the heart, mind, and soul of Randy Traywick.

Randy seems to have adjusted well, accepting his role as a country music star. It was not an easy transition, though. Sometimes he still wonders what the fuss is all about. And sometimes he craves a privacy he can never have for very long.

But it's a good life. He's made more money than he ever dreamed he'd make. He's got people paying to hear him sing. He can turn on almost any country station and hear himself. And there's always another stage to climb up on and sing, and another crowd wanting to hear him. The pressures can be almost unbearable at times, but Lib is always there looking out for him, protecting him, keeping an eye out for what is best. Although the drawbacks may seem sometimes to be overwhelming, the rewards can be overwhelming too.

Perhaps the biggest reward of all is that he can live out his life's dream every day—singing country music for a living. That sure beats frying hamburgers or raising turkeys.

CHAPTER 38

*S*o what kind of person is Randy Travis?

Those who have known him since his earliest days in Nashville describe him as polite, quiet, and a bit shy. They also talk about him being transparent—simple, direct, and honest, with no pretensions or affectations. He was always in awe of country music's greats. He loved music and he loved singing. But nobody ever talks about him showing any great ambition—in fact, most point out that Randy never exhibited any burning desire to do anything particularly. As they tell it, the ambition and burning desire always belonged to Lib.

Although he claims he hasn't changed with the success he has received in recent years, he acknowledged to reporter Chris McKain of the Rochester *Times Union* a major change from his younger days. "I was one of those kids who was always in trouble—the kind of trouble like skipping school, alcohol and drugs, breaking and entering, running from police. I got into a lot of drugs and a lot of drinking, and I look back and say, 'Why did I do those things? It couldn't have been me. I can't believe it was me.' I mean, I wouldn't rob you now if I had to, but I might've then. It just seems like it was a different person. In my case, I just think I was very rebellious. In small towns there isn't a lot to do. Some of it had to do with just running with the wrong crowd."

He has also said about himself, "I've never been a person who's planned what he's going to be doing real far in advance. I never think about things that much. I know at some point that it'll slow down. I know it's at its peak and it might not get any better than this. I look at it like this: I've been very fortunate. If it does slow down—when it does—I'll be able to handle it."

John Shaw of the Honey Grove, Texas, *Signal-Citizen* wrote in late 1986, "The most impressive indicator that he will go far in music is his candor, openness, and honesty. He obviously realizes that his success hinged on the work of a lot of people, and he recognizes that fact publicly and rewards it often. . . . When his first album went gold . . . the singer awarded complimentary plaques to all the executives, secretaries, engineers, and others who helped him make it possible."

In 1988 Bob Claypool of the Houston *Post* wrote that Randy "remains an incredibly modest, sincere, and plain old down-home nice guy. So much so that he clouds the minds of music-biz veterans who swear they've never seen anything like him. There are no temper tantrums, no bad vibes, no power plays, no flashes of ego, nothing. And there isn't a trace of phoniness, either. He is soft-spoken, courteous, and polite—a North Carolina kid who has obviously enjoyed what my mother used to call 'good raisin'.' He doesn't have any idea how big a star he is."

Russell Tarby of the Syracuse *Post-Standard* observed, "Much of his success can be traced to his sincerity. While other entertainers rely on sequins and raw sex, Travis focuses an audience's attention on his compassionate voice, rendering carefully crafted songs of heartbreak and hope. There's not a phony bone in Randy Travis's body."

Interviewing him on the road in 1987, Bob Allen found that "on this particular morning—as on most—he is affable and relaxed. But he is not especially prone to abstract theories about either the art of singing honky-tonk music or the question of his exalted position in the current musical scene."

Randy is not given to much introspection. However, with all the questions asked about himself and country music, he has been forced to come up with some answers. Mostly he's bewildered, or depends on explanations he's heard tossed around. Generally, Randy reacts to things rather than acts on them.

Shawn Ryan of the Birmingham *News* wrote, "He still has that easygoing, gosh-I-can't-believe-it charm. He's pleasant, quick to laugh. If he doesn't think very deeply about the reasons for his success, it's because he doesn't have time. He figures he'd better jump on board the gravy train while it's pulling through his station."

Randy has always been unpretentious, understated, and unaffected. But he is also stubborn and determined, with an inner self-confidence and self-awareness most people miss. He says of his early days in Nashville, "I didn't ever worry about making it. After all, I had heard all the stories about how long it took someone like Willie Nelson to finally break through. I just always believed that if I kept trying, something would happen." He has observed wryly of those early days, "I don't know why I didn't get discouraged. Lack of sense or something."

That quiet determination that few see or acknowledge manifests itself in his always doing things his own way. He would not quit and go home once he got to Nashville, he would sing only country music, and he would not compromise himself.

After the turbulent years of 1986 and 1987, he stated, "I

relax a little more, but I sure want things right. I'm a perfec-
tionist. I like the records to be right and the shows to be very
much right. I get very mad with myself when shows don't go
right, where I'm not singing a hundred percent—and you're
gonna hit a lot of those working as much as we do."

Explaining the tremendous reaction from fans toward him,
Randy noted to Chris McKain, "A lot of it is sincerity, I think.
And I've been lucky, you know, having the quality of songs that
I've had. You've heard the term, 'a standard country song'?
Well, I think that's a big part of it. That's what I'm singing. I'm
just a bad ol' boy that's made good, you know? It's hard to
figure it out. I think timing had a lot to do with it, too."

Randy loves performing and has said, "Performing is a
dream come true. It's nerve-racking to perform with someone like George or Conway. But the great thing with those
guys is they don't really care whether they sing first, last, or
in the middle. They just know how to do their job. I feel the
same way. The thing is to put on a show. It's a wonderful
feeling to go out there and know that an audience is appre-
ciating what you're doing."

He admits, "I love doing concerts, getting out there face
to face with the people who've bought my records and
made me what I am. The only reason I'm gonna cut back is
'cause you can get so steeped in things—even something
that I love as much as music—that you just need to get
away for a while to keep your life balanced."

On stage, Randy asserts, "I'm no Michael Jackson. I don't
dance and don't expect to start. I just go out and we have a
good time."

"Much of this success," observes Robert Hilburn, "is due
to the quality of his voice, a smoky, seemingly bottomless,
yet slightly nasal baritone which he bends lyrics to with an
effortless grace. In it you can detect echoes of Lefty Frizzell,
George Jones, and Merle Haggard, three major influences

Travis is compared to endlessly, and at times accused of imitating."

But Jon Pareles of the *New York Times,* in a review of *Old 8 × 10,* writes, "Mr. Travis looks to the past as a refuge, where roles are fixed and conflicts are all settled. While country once broke hearts and rocked the honky-tonks—and still can, without serious adulteration—Mr. Travis's music sits back in its easy chair and hazes over with nostalgia."

Randy's self-discipline, a key to his professional success, extends to his personal life as well. He is allergic to nearly everything, even his beloved horses—he can't be around them for several days before he sings. He can't eat a number of foods—including chocolate, which he loves—and has to carry food with him when he travels, even to foreign countries. When he must perform outside at fairs all the stuff floating in the air drives him crazy. Because of his allergies, he keeps himself on a strict regimen of exercise and healthy eating. Those close to him know that the one way assured to get him in a snit is to interfere with his workout.

In many ways he is still a boy at heart. He has simple pleasures: target shooting, horseback riding, working out, and watching TV, especially the old Andy Griffith shows. He likes home-cooked food, southern style: steak and gravy, green beans and potatoes. At five feet nine inches and 145 pounds he still has a young man's figure and, so far, hasn't had to worry about putting on weight. He likes going to the movies and listening to people like George Jones, Merle Haggard, Reba McEntire, the Judds, George Strait, and Ricky Skaggs—country artists who are not ashamed to be that way.

Down-to-earth, though a good term to describe him, leaves out something very important. Randy's talent and his success may be stratospheric, but somehow he has managed to keep his feet on the ground and his head out of the clouds. That's why his fans continue to love him even though his success has moved him farther away from them.

CHAPTER 39

A song is an arrow that pierces the heart. That's what brings so many to Nashville: the dream of being the archer who launches those arrows. Hundreds, maybe thousands, fly into Nashville on the wings of dreams. Some land already crippled. All of them learn there's much more to it than they thought, that there's more to it than just sitting on the side of your bed and making up a song that your friends like.

Everybody's going to get shot down, told no, rejected. It's what you do after you're told no that separates the winners from the losers, the ones who hang in against the ones who hang their heads and go back home. Nashville's a dream factory, but it's also a dream crusher. And for every dream that comes true, there are dozens of broken hearts. But some keep going, chasing their dreams. These pepole have made a key discovery: nobody is operating on Plan A.

Lib and Randy spent a number of years learning these

lessons over and over again. They were knocked down a number of times, but they got back up and kept going. They stuck to their dream and made some adjustments along the way. But they never gave up and trudged back home.

We look at celebrities and see ourselves. We see what we could be, should be, ought to be, want to be, but can't be. They may be somebody else, but they're singing our song, living our dream. They're finding the words for our feelings, articulating our thoughts, voicing our concerns.

Thousands across the country see Randy Travis on stage, or know Lib Hatcher's story, and want to do it too. Maybe a few will. But the plain fact is that most people don't have the guts to stick it out. It's not a lack of talent that keeps people out—it's the fire in the belly. The dogged, bull-headed persistence that keeps you going when good sense tells you to give it all up. Lib and Randy have worked harder than almost anybody else in country music. It's paid off, but people see only the glory—they don't see the sweat that's gone into it. And those two are still working hard.

Randy stayed in the news in 1989, appearing on the covers of such magazines as *Music City News, Tune-In, Country Fever,* and *Country Music.* He also made news by crossing the musicians' picket lines in Las Vegas. The American Federation of Musicians had called the strike to protest the increasing use of taped music to accompany stage acts, depriving Las Vegas musicians of their principal way to make a living. Members of the union were supposed to honor the strike, but Randy and his band elected to play their Labor Day gig at Bally's in spite of it. That act did not make him universally loved by members of the AFM or those who supported the strike.

His fourth album, *No Holding Back,* was released in September, and a Christmas album, *An Old Time Christmas,* was released in mid-November. Additionally, his duet album was coming along, with the participation of Roy Rogers, Tammy Wynette, Dolly Parton, and George Jones.

In October at the Country Music Association Awards, he watched as George Strait walked off with the top honor: Entertainer of the Year. He was still on top, but now there was a host of challengers, like Ricky Van Shelton, Clint Black, and others who were following in the path he had blazed. Some of them were getting the awards he used to win.

And there was some sadness as well. Jill Youngblood died in March in Ohio.

By the end of 1989 Lib was seeing the fruits of a vision she had long held: an organization that controlled and guided the career of Randy Travis—and perhaps other country stars—under her leadership.

Lib had been the guiding force as she and Randy formed a number of corporations to facilitate touring, performances, career direction, and investments. The umbrella organization responsible for Randy's touring is the Travis Corporation, which owns the buses and trucks that get him from town to town and has on the payroll all of the people involved with his road life. Then there is the Hatcher Corporation, which controls the merchandising and souvenirs and oversees the gift shop, although the shop was originally established as an independent entity.

Then there is the Lib Hatcher Agency, the company established in 1986 to handle Randy's bookings. With agent Alan Whitcomb at the helm, this company has plans to promote and book other country artists, including Gene Watson, whom Lib had begun managing in 1988.

Special Moments Promotions, headed by Jeff Davis, works with the agency and concert promoters, making sure all the concerts come off well. It also promotes about half of Randy's dates—the other half being promoted by state and local fairs. Lib and Randy have never forgotten what it is like to be a fan in the audience, and this company holds the heart of their operations—the live performances. It decides where and when Randy should perform. By now Randy has performed all over the United States, and wherever he goes, well, he's been there before. Special Moments makes sure the timing is right when he comes back.

There are also the publishing companies for Randy's and other songwriters' songs, administered by All Nations Music, which takes care of all the copyright and license paperwork necessary when a song is recorded and released.

Finally, there is L & R Investments, which oversees Randy and Lib's properties. They like to invest in land, reasoning that God quit making land, but He didn't quit making people. Also, it's nice to invest in something you can see and touch and walk on rather than vague portfolios of stocks and bonds that move mysteriously up and down Wall Street.

All this means that Lib is busier now than she has ever been. She's a whirlwind, in meetings or on the phone, making decisions and deals to further the career of Randy Travis. Unless there's a long tour out West or outside the U.S., Lib is generally in the office Monday through Thursday. While Randy chooses not to be as involved in all this, he is still aware of what is happening.

Lib has proven to be one of the biggest surprises in Nashville. When Randy was first signed to Warner Brothers, a number of insiders doubted she was capable of managing a budding country singer, much less a megastar. Not only has she proven them wrong in their initial assessment, but she has built a growing empire whose size and income rivals the largest companies on Music Row.

 CHAPTER *40*

"*Y*ou know, Randy is the fulfillment of all of Harold's dreams," observes a Marshville friend and neighbor. "What Randy is doing, that's what Harold always wanted to do. He's proud of Randy and all that, but it's like he resents him too. He goes around town messing things up for Randy.

"The thing about Harold is that now he thinks everybody's out to make a profit on Randy. And he thinks nobody appreciated Randy way back then and they're just trying to take advantage of him now. Well, nobody liked those boys breaking into churches and cutting gas-pump hoses and getting drunk and fighting and all that. And it's natural that when somebody from your own town, especially a town as little as Marshville, becomes a big success, well, you're proud of that. That's just human nature. But nobody's trying to take advantage of him. We love him and we're proud of him. But Harold is bound and determined to mess everything up."

Reporters from Charlotte tells stories of TV crews who have come to the house for interviews only to be run off the property by Harold on horseback, shouting threats. Some say it's because he still carries a grudge from the days when he was trying to get the boys publicity and nobody would pay him much attention. Others say that's just the way he is.

Harold has always had trouble getting along with friends and family. When Randy's paternal grandfather, Mr. Bruce, died in 1969, the story goes, Harold and his brother, Ralph, got into a fight at the funeral home over Mr. Bruce's property along the Olive Branch Road. Harold got it and Ralph didn't, causing a rift between the brothers. According to some in Marshville, Harold and Ralph never spoke to one another again, and Harold reportedly did not attend his brother's funeral in 1983.

In September 1988 Marshville declared a Randy Travis Day. A number of calls were made to Nashville, but nobody could get hold of Randy. "That woman," which is how many of the people in Marshville refer to Lib Hatcher, would come on the phone, or someone from her office would talk, but no Randy. So the organizers called Harold. They had a big plaque made up for Randy and wanted to present it to someone in the family. But Harold was on a rampage and refused to show. Ricky had agreed to come and sing, "but then Harold got ahold of him and he didn't want to cross his Daddy," so that was canceled. Finally, the day before, someone confronted Harold in town and asked why he wouldn't bring Randy's horse out for the pet show.

The next day, Harold brought Buckshot out first thing in the morning, tied him to a tree, and left him there all day without water in the hot sun. "Of course, somebody took care of him right away, but Harold went on back home," says one Marshvillian. "And you should have seen all the people—especially young kids and old people—who came just to look at Randy's horse.

"Of course we know that Randy's busy and all that, so we really couldn't expect him to come. But if he had just written on a brown paper bag, 'Thank you, Marshville. Love, Randy Travis,' it would have been worth a million dollars and been framed. I wish Randy could know that.

"Harold thinks Marshville treated Randy so bad. Well, I think Marshville has tried awfully hard to let Randy know how much it appreciates him."

In 1989 Marshville decided to honor another local who had achieved some national recognition: Regina Leigh, a member of the singing group Dave and Sugar. Marshville named a day in her honor in September. Things turned out a bit better that year—Dave and Sugar came to town and performed.

Lib Hatcher and Harold Traywick have never gotten along. Harold resents the fact that Lib gets the credit for Randy's success. "Harold thinks he's the one who made Randy Travis a country music star, not Lib Hatcher," says a Marshville friend. "He's the one who bought those boys guitars, got them lessons, and pushed them so much to play. He drove to places and spent a lot of money on them. Even paid for a recording once."

Lib is not particularly revered, for that matter, by most townspeople, who see her as the one who took him away from Marshville and keeps him away. Most agree that if it were not for her, Randy would not be where he is today—might even be doing time in prison. But these same people also resent her for erecting a barrier between Randy and Marshville, making him inaccessible to all those who'd like to call him up.

Randy loves visiting Marshville and his family, but he is in a trap: he can't just come back home and visit. Everybody wants to say hello and spend time with him, and he just doesn't have that much time to spend. He doesn't escape the celebrity spotlight in Marshville; if anything, the spotlight intensifies. And, of course, there are those who feel he should share some of his fame and success somehow. But that's impossible.

Randy became famous and successful because he worked hard and made a lot of sacrifices. But in a world where people believe that "it's not what you know, it's who you know" and that the show-biz myth of one big break catapulting someone to fame is fact, it's easy to see how folks can think that Randy can somehow make them successful too. Randy knows better, but that kind of knowledge can't be communicated to those with stars in their eyes who are convinced he has the key to open every door.

Things have changed a lot for Randy in Marshville, and visiting must serve as a reminder of what his life would have been if he had never left. Several of his boyhood friends are dead—two were shot and one died in a car wreck. His best friend from those childhood days, Tim Griffin, is serving time in prison. Some say his sentence is so long that he may never be a free man again.

Trips back home evoke some bittersweet memories for Randy. He loves visiting his family, but feels some regret he can't spend more time with them. Still, he usually calls every week. He feels good that the old place is looking better—his grandmother's house, right beside his parents' has been refurbished, and other buildings have been spruced up. A nice thing about having plenty of money is being able to help out like that back home.

But some of the other changes back there haven't been as good. Randy has felt the loss of friends and loved ones, even the loss of beloved pets, especially when Buckshot died in the summer of 1989.

EPILOGUE

*B*ack on U.S. Route 74 in the evening, heading toward Charlotte with the sunset streaming through the windshield and Marshville disappearing in the rearview mirror, I began to reflect on the Randy Travis phenomenon. What made him a star?

First, God gave the talent. That is hard to deny. Second, Harold Traywick gave him a heritage of country music, exposing him to the music and giving him guitar lessons. He pushed Randy to perform and was responsible for the first performances.

The third and fourth steps are connected: he left Marshville and he met Lib Hatcher. He had to leave Marshville to get away from the influences leading him to jail or an early death. Lib provided care and concern and a place to live. She also gave him a job and a stage where he could develop his talents. Finally, she provided management for him, an absolutely essential ingredient in any professional singer's career.

Lib Hatcher was the impetus for changing the young hoodlum Randy Traywick into Randy Travis, the country singer. To do that, she made monumental sacrifices and a monumental commitment. Randy listened to Lib and took her advice about his career. The characteristic that was so detrimental to young Randy Traywick in Marshville—the ease in which he was led, for good or ill, by others around him—turned out to be an advantage when he teamed with Lib.

Fifth, Randy and Lib made a total commitment to country music, giving up family, friends, and the security of Charlotte to take a chance in Nashville. Their commitment extended further—into their willingness to stick with frustrating, menial jobs while they pursued their dreams. Not everyone has the persistence and dogged determination to do what they did—kitchen work for over four years—without giving up and going home.

And here also lies another key: they took a long-range view of their career. They both looked far into the future and were willing to sacrifice short-term inconveniences, humiliations, and frustrations to reach their goal. Further, neither was too wrapped up in ego problems to refuse to do whatever had to be done in order to reach that goal. Both were willing to endure a myriad of small frustrations that would have sidetracked and derailed most others.

There are other factors as well. Randy really had nothing to fall back on—he could really do nothing else except sing. Being a short-order cook is not a "career"; he had nowhere to go but the stage. And he couldn't sing anything but traditional country music. He could never change directions and become a Las Vegas crooner. Combine that with his firm commitment to traditional country music and you have an integrity in both his life and performances that allowed him to persevere until his time came.

Next is his innate charisma. He's lovable, boyish, and accessible and communicates the attributes a country fan likes to see in a star. He appeals to both men and women, and even though he doesn't dance around on stage, his performances create an aura of magic when he delivers a song.

Finally, there is the aspect of timing. He was there at the right time and place for the resurgence of traditional country music. Actually, he was at the right place but the wrong time. He didn't leave, though; he stuck it out. And eventually country music came around to him.

People who are unsuccessful tend to blame their failures on "luck"; those who are successful admit to some luck, but it is a small part of the story. Randy and Lib worked hard on a career in country music, so that when luck finally poked its head in the door, they could take advantage of it.

Most people think getting to the top is the hardest thing. It's not; staying on top is even harder than getting there. And Nashville is full of one-hit wonders who had a moment in the spotlight that didn't last.

The reason Randy and Lib have managed to stay on top is because they have been willing to work hard at what they do. The same lack of ego problems that helped them endure all those early frustrations also helps them realize something else: a great singer is nothing without a good song to sing. That means respecting your listeners enough to make the effort to seek out and record the best songs you can find and the best you can write. That realization keeps Randy on the road doing shows, connected to his fans through newsletters from his fan club. It has meant long days away from home and countless autographs for hours on end.

Looking into the future is risky; even the clearest crystal ball turns cloudy. The Country Music Hall of Fame is a long way off, but it may be safe to say that Randy's headed in that direction.

Lib and Randy still disagree from time to time. He always wants to see his family more; she would rather they disappear. She's not crazy about him sending money home, but there's plenty now, so that's less of a problem. The big difficulty looming in the future will come when Randy finds a girlfriend and wants to get married and have children.

Lib will find it hard to share him, hard to accept the competition of another woman holding Randy's attention. That future female in Randy's life will probably test the relationship with Lib much more than all those hard, tough years in Nashville or even the frustrations of the Charlotte days.

Another Randy Travis song has just come on the radio. It's good to hear country radio stations playing real country music again. But right now I'd like to hear some more Randy Travis. Think I'll put on a tape of his as soon as this song is over.

BIBLIOGRAPHY

The files at the Country Music Foundation, containing a number of articles written about Randy Travis since 1985, were invaluable to my research, as were the persons I interviewed, most of whose names are mentioned in the acknowledgments.

Two books in the Union County Library in Monroe, North Carolina, proved valuable: *Sketches of Monroe and Union County* by Stack and Beasley, published in 1902, and *History of Union County* by H. Nelson Walden, published in 1964.

Information regarding the history of country music in Charlotte came from *The Charlotte Country Music Story,* published by the folklife section of the North Carolina Arts Council and the Spirit Square Arts Center of Charlotte. The most useful chapters of this booklet, whose production was directed by George Holt, were "Charlotte Country: A Sixty Year Tradition" by John Rumble, "The Piedmont Tradition" by Della Coulter, and "Recording in Charlotte: 1927–1945" by Thomas W. Hanchett.

Three general histories of country music I consulted were *Country Music, USA* by Bill C. Malone, *Tennessee Strings* by Charles Wolfe, and *The Illustrated History of Country Music,* edited by Patrick Carr. The most valuable chapter in the last book was "The Nashville Sound" by Doug Green and Bill Ivey. For the history of the music industry, the most valuable source was *American Popular Music and Its Business,* vols. 2 and 3, by Russell Sanjek.

The section on the history of the Smokies was inspired by the writings of John McPhee, with factual information from *Strangers in High Places* by Michael Frome.

Two invaluable sources for writers are *Practicing History* by Barbara Tuchman and *The Cycles of History* by Arthur Schlesinger, Jr. *A Short History of a Small Place* by T. R. Pearson, a novel about the fictional town of Neely, North Carolina, was both valuable and influential.

DISCOGRAPHY

ALBUMS:

Randy Ray Live at the Nashville Palace
Produced by Keith Stegall
Music Valley Records

"Ain't No Use"
"If It Was Love That Kept You Here"
"Free Rider"
"You Ain't Seen Nothing Yet"
"One Last Time"
"Reasons I Cheat"
"Call Somebody Who Gives a Damn"
"I Told You So"
"Promises"
"Send My Body Home (On a Freight Train)"

"Future Mister Me"
"Good Intentions"

Storms of Life
Produced by Kyle Lehning
Warner Brothers 25435-1

"On the Other Hand"*
"The Storms of Life"
"My Heart Cracked (But It Did Not Break)"
"Diggin' Up Bones"
"No Place Like Home"
"1982"
"Send My Body"
"Messin' with My Mind"
"Reasons I Cheat"*
"There'll Always Be a Honky Tonk Somewhere"

Always and Forever
Produced by Kyle Lehning
Warner Brothers 25568-1

"Too Gone Too Long"
"My House"
"Good Intentions"
"What'll You Do About Me"
"I Won't Need You Anymore"
"Forever and Ever, Amen"
"I Told You So"
"Anything"
"The Truth Is Lyin' Next to You"
"Tonight We're Gonna Tear Down the Walls"

*Produced by Kyle Lehning and Keith Stegall.

Old 8 × 10

**Produced by Kyle Lehning
Warner Brothers 25738-1**

"Honky Tonk Moon"
"Deeper Than the Holler"
"It's Out of My Hands"
"Is It Still Over?"
"Old 8 × 10"
"Written in Stone"
"The Blues in Black and White"
"Here in My Heart"
"We Ain't Out of Love Yet"
"Promises"

No Holding Back
**Produced by Kyle Lehning (except where noted)
Warner Brothers 25988-1**

"Mining for Coal"
"Singing the Blues"
"When Your World Was Turning for Me"
"He Walked on Water"
"No Stoppin' Us Now"
"It's Just a Matter of Time"*
"Card Carryin' Fool"
"Somewhere in My Broken Heart"
"Hard Rock Bottom of Your Heart"
"Have a Nice Rest of Your Life"

An Old Time Christmas
**Produced by Kyle Lehning
Warner Brothers 25972-4**

"Old Time Christmas"
"Winter Wonderland"

*Produced by Richard Perry

"Meet Me Under the Mistletoe"
"White Christmas Makes Me Blue"
"Santa Claus Is Coming to Town"
"God Rest Ye Merry Gentlemen"
"Pretty Paper"
"Oh, What a Silent Night"
"How Do I Wrap My Heart for Christmas"
"The Christmas Song"

SINGLES

"She's My Woman" (as Randy Traywick). Paula 431.
"I'll Take Any Willing Woman" b/w "Dreamin'" (as Randy
    Traywick). Paula 432
"On the Other Hand" b/w "Can't Stop Now." Warner
    Brothers 28962.
"1982" b/w "Reasons I Cheat." Warner Brothers 28828.
"Diggin' Up Bones" b/w "There'll Always Be a Honky Tonk
    Somewhere." Warner Brothers 28649.
"No Place Like Home" b/w "Send My Body." Warner
    Brothers 28525.
"Forever and Ever, Amen" b/w "Promises." Warner Brothers
    28384.
"I Won't Need You Anymore" b/w "Tonight I'm Walkin' Out
    on the Blues." Warner Brothers 28246.
"Too Gone Too Long" b/w "My House." Warner Brothers
    28286.
"Honky Tonk Moon" b/w "Young Guns." Warner Brothers
    27833.
"I Told You So" b/w "Good Intentions." Warner Brothers
    27969.
"Is It Still Over?" b/w "Here in my Heart." Warner Brothers
    27551.
"Promises" b/w "Written in Stone." Warner Brothers 22917.
"It's Just a Matter of Time" b/w "This Day Was Made for Me
    and You." Warner Brothers 28841.

 Index

Academy of Country Music Awards, 87–92, 117, 122, 125, 133
"Act Naturally," 52
Acuff, Roy, 36, 49, 51, 60, 115, 168
Acuff-Rose Publishing, 49
"Ain't No Use," 54, 55, 64, 95
Alabama, 41, 44, 58, 88, 89, 122, 150, 158
"All My Trials," 113
All Nations Music, 188
Allen, Bob, 182
Always and Forever, 122–124, 137, 141, 147–149, 152, 167
"Always Late," 78
American Federation of Musicians, 50, 186
American Music Awards, 121, 148, 167
American Music Operators Association, 147
Anderson, Bill, 9, 54

Anderson, John, 58, 70, 74
"Anything," 123
"Are You Lonesome Tonight," 10
Arnold, Eddy, 9, 49, 60, 94
ASCAP, 72, 88
Asleep at the Wheel, 168
"Austin City Limits," 114
Autry, Gene, 143
Azrak, Janice, 89, 140

Bandy, Moe, 145
Bane, Michael, 85
Barnes, Max, 98, 123
"Battle of New Orleans," 9
Beatles, 30, 55
Bell, Ken, 153
Big Bopper, 10
Billboard, 30, 58, 98, 122, 137
Black, Clint, 187
Blackmon, Buddy, 82
Bluegrass Boys, 36
"Blues in Black and White," 153

Index

"Born a Woman," 70
Bowen, Jimmy, 52, 70, 71
Bradley, Harold, 48–50
Bradley, Owen, 48–50, 57
"Branded Man," 56
Brawner, Debbie, 65
Briarhoppers, 12, 36–38
Brockman, Polk, 35, 36
Brooks, Karen, 70
Brower Brothers, 63–64
Brown, Floyd, 54
Brown, T. Graham, 87, 89
Burnette, Billy, 87
Byrd, Stan, 31, 39, 52

"Call Somebody Who Gives a
    Damn," 56
"Can't Stop Now," 95
Capitol Records, 38
"Carrying Fire," 74
Carson, Fiddlin' John, 35
Carter, Gary, 93
Carter Family, 36, 38
Cash, Johnny, 9
Cash, Roseanne, 44, 51
Castle Studios, 49
CBS Publishing, 41–42, 71
Cedarwood Publishing, 49, 50
Chapman, Tracy, 168
Charlie Daniels Band, 44
Charlotte, N.C., beginning of
    country music in, 30, 35–38
Chase, Charlie, 65
Clanton, Darrell, 68
Clark, Dick, 88
Claypool, Bob, 118, 181
Cline, Patsy, 11, 49, 89, 151
Coe, Marvin, 123
Coley, John Ford, 75
Collins, Tommy, 64
Colter, Jessie, 44
"Come Back When You Grow Up,"
    71
Conley, Earl Thomas, 58, 111
Cooper, George, 49–50
Country City USA, 21, 22, 26, 27,
    29, 31, 33

Country music, 30, 35–38, 44–45,
    48–51, 58–62, 65–67
  awards, 9, 51, 58, 87–98,
      109–111, 114, 117, 118,
      121–122, 147–149, 152,
      162, 167–168, 176–177,
      187
  new traditionalism in, 71,
      127–129
Country Music Association (CMA),
    50, 61, 69, 71
  awards, 58, 109–111, 114, 118,
      147, 152, 162, 187
Country Music Foundation, 129
Country Music Hall of Fame, 51,
    52, 147, 195
Country radio, 37–38, 59–60
  See also Nashville Network
Country Radio Seminar, 86
Creel, Vincent, 149
Crutchfield, Charles, 37
Crystal, Billy, 168
Curb Records, 43

"Dark as a Dungeon," 78
Dave and Sugar, 191
Davis, Jeff, 160, 187
Davis, Jimmie, 38
Davis, Mac, 44, 88
Davis, Paul, 111
Davis, Skeeter, 9
Decca Records, 36
"Deeper Than the Holler," 152
Delmore Brothers, 36
Denver, John, 44
Dickens, Little Jimmie, 85
"Diggin' Up Bones," 99, 109, 115,
    116, 123
Dimension Recording Studio, 21
"Does Fort Worth Ever Cross Your
    Mind," 59, 89
Don't Cheat in Our Home Town,
    59
Dorff, Steve, 74
Douglas, Charlie, 81
Douglas, Jerry, 122
Dr. Hook, 42

Index

"Dreamin'," 30
"Drivin' My Life Away," 45
Durham, Hal, 113

Eagles, 44
Edwards, Joe, 95
"El Paso," 9
Elektra Records, 71
"Elvira," 45
Emery, Ralph, 39, 63–65, 67, 77, 78, 116, 163–164, 169
England Dan, 75
Epic Records, 75
Everette, Leon, 42
Everly Brothers, 14

Fair, Mark, 157
Fan Fair, 79–81, 147, 160, 169, 176
Fans and fan clubs, 59, 67, 79–81, 97–98, 112, 114, 129, 131, 147, 149, 158, 160–161, 169–171, 173–174, 176–179, 183, 184
First Edition, 75
"Forever and Ever, Amen," 122, 123, 147–149
Forrester Sisters, 122
"Free Rider," 55
Fricke, Janie, 58
Frizzell, David, 70
Frizzell, Lefty, 60, 78, 82, 132, 158, 183
"Future Mister Me," 56

Gamble, Dixie, 71
"Gambler," 76
Gantt, Harvey, 112
Gardner, JoAnne, 51
Gatlin, Larry, 44
Gayle, Crystal, 70
Gibson, Don, 9
Gilley, Mickey, 42, 44, 58, 119
Glaser Brothers Studio, 75
Gold Albums and Records, 44, 45, 51, 113, 133
Goldsmith, Tommy, 84, 156

"Good Hearted Woman," 95, 119
"Good Intentions," 56, 123
Gore, Al, 123
"Got No Reason Now for Going Home," 77
Grammy Awards, 9, 51, 121–122, 148, 168
Grand Ole Opry, 25, 37, 39, 45, 48–51, 54, 61, 65–67, 72, 85–86, 113–115, 117, 134, 145, 147, 150, 176
"Grand Tour," 14
Greenwood, Lee, 42, 58
Griffin, Tim, 17, 192
Grosswendt, Martin, 155

Haggard, Merle, 30, 55, 56, 58, 77, 80, 95, 99, 119, 123, 125, 128, 129, 132, 139, 143, 150, 183, 184
Hanks, Tom, 151
"Happy Trails," 162
Harper, Carol, 137
Harper, John, 21, 22, 26, 30, 33
Harris, Emmylou, 44, 70
Harris, Judy, 71
Hartman, Dick, 37
Hatcher, Lib, 21–33, 39–43, 45–48, 51–57, 62–68, 72–73, 79–85, 89–95, 99, 100, 111, 113, 119, 124–127, 132–134, 137, 140–142, 145, 147, 151, 160–168, 173–174, 177, 180, 185–188, 190–196
"He Stopped Loving Her Today," 95
"Heaven's Gonna Miss You Tonight," 81
"Hee Haw," 111, 151
Henley, Larry, 153
"Here in My Heart," 153
"Hickory Hollow's Tramp," 56
Higdon, Pat, 76
Highway 101, 169
Hilburn, Robert, 151, 155, 158, 183
Hill and Range Publishers, 49

Index

Hobbs, John, 45, 46, 55, 132
Holden, Stephen, 150
Holly, Buddy, 10
"Home Sweet Home," 99
"Honky Tonk Moon," 152
Horn, Richard, 94
Horton, Johnny, 9
"Hungry Eyes," 56
Hunley, Con, 31
Hunter, Nick, 73, 96–97
"Hurricane," 42
Hurst, Jack, 129

"I Feel Fine," 55
"I Love a Rainy Night," 45
"I Saw the Light," 12, 13, 119
"I Told You So," 42, 56, 64, 68, 81,
    123, 148, 167
"I Won't Need You Anymore," 123
"I'd Really Love to See You
    Tonight," 75
"If It Was Love That Kept You
    Here," 55
Iglesias, Julio, 58
"I'll Fly Away," 64
"I'll Take Any Willing Woman," 30
"I'm So Lonesome I Could Cry," 85
"Is It Still Over?" 153
"It's Out of My Hands," 153
"I've Been Around Enough to
    Know," 95
Ivey, Bill, 129

Jackson, Michael, 162, 168, 183
Jaeger, Barbara, 156
Jarreau, Al, 42
Jenkins, Carl, 49
Jenkins, DeWitt "Snuffy," 36
Jennings, Waylon, 44, 75, 99, 119
Jim and Jesse, 115
Johnson, David, 93
Jones, George, 9, 13, 14, 44, 77,
    80, 93, 112, 115, 117, 125, 128,
    129, 132, 139, 150, 158, 177,
    183, 184, 187
Jordan, Bill, 26
Judds, 58, 76, 88, 150, 168, 184

Kerns, William, 119
Kingston Trio, 9
Kristofferson, Kris, 111

lang, k.d., 168
Lanson, Snooky, 49
Larson, Nicolette, 111
Lee, Dickie, 64
Lee, Johnny, 70
Lehning, Kyle, 74–76, 82, 97, 124
Leigh, Regina, 191
"Let's Chase Each Other Round the
    Room," 95, 119, 123
"Let's Fall to Pieces Together," 59,
    64
Lindley, John, 126, 153
"Little Good News," 58
"Little Old Log Cabin in the Lane,"
    35
"Lonely Nights," 42
"Lonely Shadow," 11
"Lost in the Fifties," 89, 122
"Louisiana Saturday Night," 114,
    119
Loveless, Patty, 112
Lovett, Lyle, 168
Lynn, Loretta, 26, 44, 49, 147

Macon, Uncle Dave, 36
Maddox, David, 42
Mainer's Mountaineers, 36, 37
"Mama He's Crazy," 58
"Mama Tried," 56
Mama Wynette, 31, 56, 81
Mandrell, Barbara, 44, 58, 63, 64,
    83, 84, 93, 149, 177
Mandrell, Irlene, 177
Mandrell, Louise, 177
Mangum, Jimmy, 12
Mangum, Kate, 11–12
Marlboro Country Music Tour, 150
Marshville, N.C., 1, 6–9, 16–19,
    22, 28, 53, 114–115, 136,
    143–144, 191–192
Mattea, Kathy, 116, 177
Maynard, Carrie, 159
MCA Records, 71

Index

McAnally, Mac, 153
McCarters, 152
McCready, Mary Ann, 69
McDaniel, Mel, 119
McDowell, Ronnie, 93
McEntire, Reba, 88, 122, 149, 168, 184
McFerrin, Bobby, 168
McKain, Chris, 180, 183
Merlis, Bob, 80
"Messin' with My Mind," 99
Michael, George, 162, 167, 168
"Midnight Girl in a Sunset Town," 76
Milsap, Ronnie, 44, 75, 89, 122
Money, Rick Wayne, 93
Monk, Charlie, 41–43, 51, 55, 71, 72, 75, 86, 132–133
Monroe, Bill, 36, 168
Morgan, George, 9
Morgan, Lorrie, 77, 115
Morris, Gary, 41, 70, 74, 140
Morrison, Cameron, 36
Murphey, Michael Martin, 58
Murray, Anne, 44, 58
Music City News, 140, 186
    awards, 122, 147, 149, 176
Music Country Radio Network, 81
Music Row, 39, 45, 50–52, 59–61, 65–67, 70, 71, 79, 84, 85, 98, 111, 134, 136, 140, 188
"My Heart Cracked (But It Did Not Break)," 98, 119
"My House," 123

Nashville, beginning of country music in, 38, 44–45, 48–51
Nashville Network (TNN), 45, 54, 63, 65, 67, 115, 119, 140, 149, 168
"Nashville Now," 63–65, 77–78, 116, 140, 163
Nashville Palace, 45–47, 52, 54–57, 63–65, 67, 72, 75, 76, 81, 83, 85, 119, 132–133, 146
Nashville Songwriters Association Awards, 121

Nashville Sound, 49, 50
National Association of Recording Arts and Sciences, 51
Nelson, Willie, 44, 58, 75, 111, 119, 182
Newton, Juice, 44, 111
Nights Are Forever without You, 75
"Nine to Five," 45
"1982," 82, 83, 86, 95, 96, 99, 117
Nitty Gritty Dirt Band, 70, 74
No Holding Back, 186
"No Place Like Home," 99, 116
Norman, Jim Ed, 70, 136–137

Oak Ridge Boys, 44, 88
O'Connor, Mark, 122
Oermann, Robert, 153–154, 159
Okeh Records, 35, 36
Old 8 × 10, 152–153, 160, 168, 184
"Old Hen Cackled and the Rooster's Going to Crow," 35
Old Time Christmas, 186
"On the Other Hand," 74, 76, 77, 80–83, 86, 89, 95–98, 109, 113, 121, 123
"One Last Time," 56
Opryland, 45, 67, 109
    See also Grand Ole Opry
Orbison, Roy, 168
Oslin, K. T., 168
Osmond, Marie, 111
Ossoff, Robert, 125
Overstreet, Paul, 76, 116, 123, 149, 152
Owens, Buck, 168, 169

Pamper Publishers, 49
Pappas, Angelo, 25
Pareles, Jon, 184
Parkie, Monty, 161
Parton, Dolly, 44, 45, 162, 187
Paula Records, 30, 43
Pearl, Minnie, 168
Peer, Ralph, 35, 36
People's Choice Awards, 168

Index

Peter, Paul, and Mary, 70
Pierce, Webb, 9
Pillow, Ray, 45, 46
Pistilli, Gene, 153
Platinum Albums, 51, 121
Pointer, Anita, 111
Polyfox Studio, 56
Posey, Sandy, 70
"Prairie Rose," 74, 77
Presley, Elvis, 10, 113, 151, 172
Price, Ray, 9, 70, 94
Pride, Charlie, 44
"Promises," 43, 56, 153, 177
Pruett, Jeanne, 81

Rabbitt, Eddie, 44, 45, 70, 111
Ragsdale, John, 43
Randy Ray Live at the Nashville Palace, 55–57, 75
Randy Travis Day, 112, 190
Rasmussen, Bonnie, 39
Ray, Randy, 47, 54–57, 63–64, 71, 73, 75
    changes name to Travis, 73
RCA Victor, 36, 38, 49, 50
"Reason I Came," 11
"Reasons I Cheat," 56, 74, 95, 99
Recording Industry Association of America, 51
Reed, Jerry, 45
Reeves, Jim, 9, 94
Reynolds, George, 49
Right or Wrong, 59
Ritchie, Lionel, 111
Ritter, Tex, 143
Rivelli, Tommy, 93
Robbins, Marty, 9
Robertson, Hill, 24, 25
Rocco, Tommy, 64
"Rockin' with the Rhythm of the Rain," 76
Rodgers, Jimmie, 36, 51, 99
Rodman, Judy, 88, 111
Rogers, Kenny, 44, 58, 75, 76
Rogers, Roy, 161–162, 187
Rose, Fred, 49, 51

Rosen, Johnny, 55
Ross, Robert, 157
Ruffin, Gail, 137–138
Ruffin, Travis, 137–138
Russell, Johnny, 52, 64, 77, 85
Rustler's Rhapsody, 74, 77
Ryan, Shawn, 182
Ryman Auditorium, 49, 66, 86

Sales, Jim, 123
Schlitz, Don, 76, 123, 149, 152, 153
Schneider, John, 88
Schwarzenegger, Arnold, 168
Scott, Lang, 54
Scruggs, Earl, 36
Seals, Dan, 75
Seals, Troy, 98, 123
"Send My Body Home (On a Freight Train)," 56, 63, 95, 99
"Settin' the Woods on Fire," 123
Sexton, Drew, 93, 161
"Sexy Eyes," 42
Sharp, Martha, 69–73, 75, 76, 80–82, 97, 124
Shaw, John, 181
"She's a Woman," 30
"She's My Woman," 30
Shelton, Aaron, 49
Sheppard, T. G., 44, 70, 83
Shriver, Evelyn, 137, 139–142, 151, 174
Silverstein, Shel, 75
"Sing Me Back Home," 56
"Single Girl," 70
"Sixteen Tons," 78
Skaggs, Ricky, 58, 59, 71, 109, 115, 183
Smith, Arthur, 14
Smith, Bruce Lee, 114
Snider, Mike, 77
Special Moments Promotions, 160–161, 187
Staley, Lawrence, 24, 25
Stampley, Joe, 30, 145
Statler Brothers, 44, 93, 149, 177

Index

Stegall, Keith, 39, 41–43, 52, 55, 56, 64, 72, 74–76, 81, 119
Stevens, Ray, 177
Stoner, George, 29
Storms of Life, 98–100, 109, 113, 116, 121, 124, 133, 137, 141
Strait, George, 59, 64, 71, 88, 89, 93, 97, 118, 149, 150, 184, 187
Stuart, Marty, 87
Sweet Dreams, 89
Sweethearts of the Rodeo, 76

Tant, Ann, 31, 41, 47, 52, 56, 81, 132–134
Tarby, Russell, 181
Tassel, Jerry, 30
Tassel, Van, 30
Tennessee Ramblers, 37
Texas Troubadours, 99
Thacker, Rocky, 93
"There'll Always Be a Honky Tonk Somewhere," 99
Thompson, Hank, 9
Three Story Music Publishers, 133
Tillis, Mel, 111
Tillis, Pam, 70, 74
TNN, *see* Nashville Network (TNN)
"To All the Girls I've Loved Before," 58
"Tom Dooley," 9
"Tonight We're Gonna Tear Down the Walls," 123
"Too Gone Too Long," 122, 147
Travis, Merle, 78, 99
Travis, Randy
  albums, 55–57, 98–100, 122–124, 152–153, 186
  awards, 87–89, 109–111, 117, 121–122, 147–149, 162, 167–168, 176–177
  body building, 52, 111, 140, 161, 168
  childhood and education, 8, 11–23, 143–144
  club dates, 83–85, 92–95

European and USO tours, 152, 162
fan club, 160–161
father, relations with, 3, 14–17, 27–28, 143, 145, 189
at Grand Ole Opry, 85–86, 113–115
guitar lessons, 12, 145, 146
hometown visits, 53, 114–115, 136, 191–192
horses, 17, 136–138, 157, 160, 190, 192
interviews and media coverage, 84, 89–95, 115–120, 127–130, 132, 149–152, 155–159, 162–165, 180–184, 186
and Lib Hatcher, 21–23, 31–32, 145, 163–166
movie role, 125–126
name change, 47, 73, 77
as Randy Ray, 47, 54–57, 63–64, 71, 73, 75
recordings, early, 30, 43, 54–57, 72
reviews, 94, 113, 114, 116, 119–120, 150, 153–154, 173, 181–184
stardom, problems of, 130–135, 157, 159, 161, 170–175, 179
talent contests, 13–15, 20–21, 27, 54, 145
television appearances, 63–65, 77–78, 111, 115, 116, 119, 140, 148, 150–151, 167
video, 116–117
Warner Brothers, first recording, 74, 77, 81–82, 96
Traywick, Bobbie Rose (mother), 2–4, 8, 13, 16–19, 27, 126, 145, 160
Traywick, David (brother), 8, 12, 13, 19
Traywick, Dennis (brother), 8, 160
Traywick, Harold (father), 1–6, 8–9, 11–19, 21, 22, 27, 28, 90,

Traywick, Harold (*cont.*)
    126, 143–145, 160, 189–191,
    193
Traywick, Randy, *see* Travis, Randy
Traywick, Ricky (brother), 8,
    12–14, 16, 18, 19, 21, 145, 190
Tree Publishers, 49
"Truth Is Lyin' Next to You," 123
Tubb, Ernest, 9, 11, 49, 99, 143,
    169
Twitty, Conway, 44, 56, 59, 70, 93,
    139, 147, 156, 177, 183

"Uncle Pen," 59
Urban Cowboy, 29, 44

Valens, Richie, 10
Van Shelton, Ricky, 168, 177, 187
Vee, Bobby, 71
Viewer's Choice Awards, 149, 168
Vipperman, Vip, 82

Wagoner, Porter, 9
"Waltz across Texas," 95
Wariner, Steve, 89, 111
Warner Brothers Records, 31,
    68–72, 74, 75, 77, 80–83,
    89–91, 96–97, 113, 117, 121,
    133, 136, 140, 147, 161, 178,
    188
Watson, Gene, 26, 77, 187
Wayne, John, 74
Wayne, Patrick, 74
WBT Radio, Charlotte, 37–38
"We Ain't Out of Love Yet," 153
"We're in This Love Together," 42
Wells, Kitty, 9, 49, 89
West, Dottie, 26
West, Shelly, 70

"What'll You Do About Me," 123
Whitcomb, Alan, 187
White, Danny, 111
"White Christmas Makes Me Blue,"
    114
"White Lightning," 9
Whitehurst, Jerry, 78
Whites, 115
Whitley, Keith, 87
"Who's Gonna Fill Their Shoes,"
    115
"Why Not Me," 58
Wiggins, Little Roy, 60
Williams, Hank, 12, 33, 34, 49, 51,
    60, 85, 95, 113, 119, 123, 125,
    132, 143
Williams, Hank, Jr., 44, 70, 149,
    158
Wills, Bob, 99, 123
"Wind beneath My Wings," 58
Winfrey, Juanita, 137
Winwood, Steve, 168
"Workin' Man," 55
"Written in Stone," 153
WSM Radio, Nashville, 37, 45, 49,
    51, 65, 67
WSOC Radio, Charlotte, 21, 22, 26
Wynette, Tammy, 165, 187

Yoakam, Dwight, 78, 168, 169
"You Ain't Seen Nothing Yet," 54,
    56
Young, Faron, 9
Young Guns, 125–126
Youngblood, Jill, 147, 161, 162,
    187
"Your Hit Parade," 49
Youth Yellow Pages, 167